The USES of
the UNIVERSITY

The Godkin Lectures
at Harvard University
1963

The Godkin Lectures on the Essentials of
Free Government and the Duties of the Citizen
were established at Harvard University in 1903
in memory of Edwin Lawrence Godkin (1831–1902).
They are given annually under the auspices of the
Harvard Graduate School of Public Administration.

The USES of the UNIVERSITY

CLARK KERR

President of the University of California

Harvard University Press
Cambridge, Massachusetts
1963

FOREWORD

Universities in America are at a hinge of history: while connected with their past, they are swinging in another direction. This volume, based on the 1963 Godkin Lectures, delivered at Harvard University on April 23, 24, and 25, 1963, attempts to describe and to evaluate some of the significant new developments in American higher education. The title, "The Uses of the University," implies a generally optimistic tone, for it is not the *misuses* of the university that will mainly concern us. At the same time, however, it is well to note that in the discussion that follows, analysis should not be confused with approval or description with defense.

Although it is one of our oldest social institutions, the university today finds itself in a quite novel position in society. It faces its new role with few precedents to fall back on, with little but platitudes to mask the nakedness of the change. Instead of platitudes and nostalgic glances backward to what it once was, the university needs a rigorous look at the reality of the world it occupies today.

The basic reality, for the university, is the widespread recognition that new knowledge is the most important factor in economic and social growth. We are just now perceiving that the university's invisible product, knowledge, may be the most powerful single element in our culture, affecting the rise and fall of professions and even of social classes, of regions and even of nations.

Because of this fundamental reality, the university is being called upon to produce knowledge as never before—for civic and regional purposes, for national purposes, and even for no purpose at all beyond the realization that most knowledge eventually comes to serve mankind. And it is also being called upon to transmit knowledge to an unprecedented proportion of the population.

This reality is reshaping the very nature and quality of the university. Old concepts of faculty-student relations, of research, of faculty-administration roles are being changed at a rate without parallel. And this at a time when it seems that an entire generation is pounding at the gates and demanding admission. To the academician, conservative by nature, the sound made by the new generation often resembles the howl of a mob. To the politician, it is a signal to be obeyed. To the administrator, it is a warning that we are in new times and that the decisions we make now will be uncommonly productive—both of good and ill.

Thus the university has come to have a new centrality for all of us, as much for those who never see the ivied halls as for those who pass through them or reside there.

The university has been a remarkably unstudied institution until very recently. Seymour Harris was one of the first of my fellow economists to examine education as one might any other activity of society and to subject it to economic analysis. Today education, including higher education, is being scrutinized in all its aspects. This reflects the increasing recognition of its uses in economic growth, in international competition, in political and social as well as cultural development. One can only wonder whether the university was a better place before people began writing and talking so much about it—before they became so conscious of its uses.

CLARK KERR

Berkeley, California
June 12, 1963

CONTENTS

1 The Idea of a Multiversity 1

2 The Realities of the Federal Grant
University 46

3 The Future of the City of Intellect 85

Notes 127

Index 137

The USES of
the UNIVERSITY

I

THE IDEA OF
A MULTIVERSITY

THE university started as a single community—a community of masters and students. It may even be said to have had a soul in the sense of a central animating principle. Today the large American university is, rather, a whole series of communities and activities held together by a common name, a common governing board, and related purposes. This great transformation is regretted by some, accepted by many, gloried in, as yet, by few. But it should be understood by all.

The university of today can perhaps be understood, in part, by comparing it with what it once was—with the academic cloister of Cardinal Newman, with the research organism of Abraham Flexner. Those are the ideal types from which it has derived, ideal types which still constitute the illusions of some of its inhabitants. The modern American university, however, is not Oxford nor is it

Berlin; it is a new type of institution in the world. As a new type of institution, it is not really private and it is not really public; it is neither entirely of the world nor entirely apart from it. It is unique.

"The Idea of a University" was, perhaps, never so well expressed as by Cardinal Newman when engaged in founding the University of Dublin a little over a century ago.[1] His views reflected the Oxford of his day whence he had come. A university, wrote Cardinal Newman, is "the high protecting power of all knowledge and science, of fact and principle, of inquiry and discovery, of experiment and speculation; it maps out the territory of the intellect, and sees that . . . there is neither encroachment nor surrender on any side." He favored "liberal knowledge," and said that "useful knowledge" was a "deal of trash."

Newman was particularly fighting the ghost of Bacon who some 250 years before had condemned "a kind of adoration of the mind . . . by means whereof men have withdrawn themselves too much from the contemplation of nature, and the observations of experience, and have tumbled up and down in their own reason and conceits." Bacon believed that knowledge should be for the benefit and use of men, that it should "not be as a courtesan, for pleasure and vanity only, or as a bond-woman, to acquire and gain to her master's use; but as a spouse, for generation, fruit and comfort."[2]

To this Newman replied that "Knowledge is

capable of being its own end. Such is the constitution of the human mind, that any kind of knowledge, if it really be such, is its own reward." And in a sharp jab at Bacon he said: "The Philosophy of Utility, you will say, Gentlemen, has at least done its work; and I grant it—it aimed low, but it has fulfilled its aim." Newman felt that other institutions should carry on research, for "If its object were scientific and philosophical discovery, I do not see why a University should have any students"—an observation sardonically echoed by today's students who often think their professors are not interested in them at all but only in research. A University training, said Newman, "aims at raising the intellectual tone of society, at cultivating the public mind, at purifying the national taste, at supplying true principles to popular enthusiasm and fixed aims to popular aspirations, at giving enlargement and sobriety to the ideas of the age, at facilitating the exercise of political powers, and refining the intercourse of private life." It prepares a man "to fill any post with credit, and to master any subject with facility."

This beautiful world was being shattered forever even as it was being so beautifully portrayed. By 1852, when Newman wrote, the German universities were becoming the new model. The democratic and industrial and scientific revolutions were all well underway in the western world. The gentleman "at home in any society" was soon to be at home in none. Science was beginning to take the place of moral philosophy, research the place of teaching.

"The Idea of a Modern University," to use Flexner's phrase,[3] was already being born. "A University," said Flexner in 1930, "is not outside, but inside the general social fabric of a given era. . . . It is not something apart, something historic, something that yields as little as possible to forces and influences that are more or less new. It is on the contrary . . . an expression of the age, as well as an influence operating upon both present and future."

It was clear by 1930 that "Universities have changed profoundly—and commonly in the direction of the social evolution of which they are part." This evolution had brought departments into universities, and still new departments; institutes and ever more institutes; created vast research libraries; turned the philosopher on his log into a researcher in his laboratory or the library stacks; taken medicine out of the hands of the profession and put it into the hands of the scientists; and much more. Instead of the individual student, there were the needs of society; instead of Newman's eternal "truths in the natural order," there was discovery of the new; instead of the generalist, there was the specialist. The university became, in the words of Flexner, "an institution consciously devoted to the pursuit of knowledge, the solution of problems, the critical appreciation of achievement and the training of men at a really high level." No longer could a single individual "master any subject"—Newman's universal liberal man was gone forever.

But as Flexner was writing of the "Modern University," it, in turn, was ceasing to exist. The Berlin of Humboldt was being violated just as Berlin had violated the soul of Oxford. The universities were becoming too many things. Flexner himself complained that they were "secondary schools, vocational schools, teacher-training schools, research centers, 'uplift' agencies, businesses—these and other things simultaneously." They engaged in "incredible absurdities," "a host of inconsequential things." They "needlessly cheapened, vulgarized and mechanized themselves." Worst of all, they became " 'service stations' for the general public."

Even Harvard. "It is clear," calculated Flexner, "that of Harvard's total expenditures not more than one-eighth is devoted to the *central* university disciplines at the level at which a university ought to be conducted." He wondered: "Who has forced Harvard into this false path? No one. It does as it pleases; and this sort of thing pleases." It obviously did not please Flexner. He wanted Harvard to disown the Graduate School of Business and let it become, if it had to survive it all, the "Boston School of Business." He would also have banished all Schools of Journalism and Home Economics, football, correspondence courses, and much else.

It was not only Harvard and other American universities, but also London. Flexner asked "in what

sense the University of London is a university at all."
It was only "a federation."

By 1930, American universities had moved a long
way from Flexner's "Modern University" where
"The heart of a university is a graduate school of
arts and sciences, the solidly professional schools
(mainly, in America, medicine and law) and certain
research institutes." They were becoming less and
less like a "genuine university," by which Flexner
meant "an organism, characterized by highness and
definiteness of aim, unity of spirit and purpose." The
"Modern University" was as nearly dead in 1930
when Flexner wrote about it, as the old Oxford was
in 1852 when Newman idealized it. History moves
faster than the observer's pen. Neither the ancient
classics and theology nor the German philosophers
and scientists could set the tone for the really modern
university—the multiversity.

"The Idea of a Multiversity" has no bard to sing
its praises; no prophet to proclaim its vision; no
guardian to protect its sanctity. It has its critics, its
detractors, its transgressors. It also has its barkers
selling its wares to all who will listen—and many
do. But it also has its reality rooted in the logic of
history. It is an imperative rather than a reasoned
choice among elegant alternatives.

President Nathan Pusey wrote in his latest annual
report to the members of the Harvard Board of
Overseers that the average date of graduation of the
present Board members was 1924; and much has

happened to Harvard since 1924. Half of the buildings are new. The faculty has grown five-fold, the
budget nearly fifteen-fold. "One can find almost
anywhere one looks similar examples of the effect
wrought in the curriculum and in the nature of the
contemporary university by widening international
awareness, advancing knowledge, and increasingly
sophisticated methods of research. . . . Asia and
Africa, radio telescopes, masers and lasers and devices for interplanetary exploration unimagined in
1924—these and other developments have effected
such enormous changes in the intellectual orientation and aspiration of the contemporary university
as to have made the university we knew as students
now seem a strangely underdeveloped, indeed a
very simple and an almost unconcerned kind of
institution. And the pace of change continues."[4]

Not only at Harvard. The University of California
last year had operating expenditures from all sources
of nearly half a billion dollars, with almost another
100 million for construction; a total employment of
over 40,000 people, more than IBM and in a far
greater variety of endeavors; operations in over a
hundred locations, counting campuses, experiment
stations, agricultural and urban extension centers,
and projects abroad involving more than fifty countries; nearly 10,000 courses in its catalogues; some
form of contact with nearly every industry, nearly
every level of government, nearly every person in
its region. Vast amounts of expensive equipment

were serviced and maintained. Over 4,000 babies were born in its hospitals. It is the world's largest purveyor of white mice. It will soon have the world's largest primate colony. It will soon also have 100,000 students—30,000 of them at the graduate level; yet much less than one third of its expenditures are directly related to teaching. It already has nearly 200,000 students in extension courses—including one out of every three lawyers and one out of every six doctors in the state. And Harvard and California are illustrative of many more.

Newman's "Idea of a University" still has its devotees—chiefly the humanists and the generalists and the undergraduates. Flexner's "Idea of a Modern University" still has its supporters—chiefly the scientists and the specialists and the graduate students. "The Idea of a Multiversity" has its practitioners—chiefly the administrators, who now number many of the faculty among them, and the leadership groups in society at large. The controversies are still around in the faculty clubs and the student coffee houses; and the models of Oxford and Berlin and modern Harvard all animate segments of what was once a "community of masters and students" with a single vision of its nature and purpose. These several competing visions of true purpose, each relating to a different layer of history, a different web of forces, cause much of the malaise in the university communities of today. The university is so many things to so many different people that it must, of necessity, be partially at war with itself.

How did the multiversity happen? No man created it; in fact, no man visualized it. It has been a long time coming about and it has a long way to go. What is its history? How is it governed? What is life like within it? What is its justification? Does it have a future?

THE STRANDS OF HISTORY

The multiversity draws on many strands of history. To the extent that its origins can be identified, they can be traced to the Greeks. But there were several traditions even then. Plato had his Academy devoted to truth largely for its own sake, but also truth for the philosophers who were to be kings. The Sophists, whom Plato detested so much that he gave them an evil aura persisting to this day, had their schools too. These schools taught rhetoric and other useful skills—they were more interested in attainable success in life than they were in the unattainable truth. The Pythagoreans were concerned, among other things, with mathematics and astronomy. The modern academician likes to trace his intellectual forebears to the groves of Academe; but the modern university with its professional schools and scientific institutes might look equally to the Sophists and the Pythagoreans. The humanists, the professionals, and the scientists all have their roots in ancient times. The "Two Cultures" or the "Three Cultures" are almost as old as culture itself.

Despite its Greek precursors, however, the university is, as Hastings Rashdall wrote, "a distinctly medieval institution."[5] In the Middle Ages it developed many of the features that prevail today— a name and a central location, masters with a degree of autonomy, students, a system of lectures, a procedure for examinations and degrees, and even an administrative structure with its "faculties." Salerno in medicine, Bologna in law, and Paris in theology and philosophy were the great pacesetters. The university came to be a center for the professions, for the study of the classics, for theological and philosophical disputes. Oxford and Cambridge, growing out of Paris, developed in their distinctive ways with their particular emphasis on the residential college instead of the separate faculties as the primary unit.

By the end of the eighteenth century the European universities had long since become oligarchies, rigid in their subject matter, centers of reaction in their societies—opposed, in large part, to the Reformation, unsympathetic to the spirit of creativity of the Renaissance, antagonistic to the new science. There was something almost splendid in their disdain for contemporary events. They stood like castles without windows, profoundly introverted. But the tides of change can cut very deep. In

France the universities were swept away by the Revolution, as they almost had been in England at the time of Cromwell.

It was in Germany that the rebirth of the university took place. Halle had dropped teaching exclusively in Latin in 1693; Göttingen had started the teaching of history in 1736; but it was the establishment of Berlin by Wilhelm von Humboldt in 1809 from his vantage point in the Prussian Ministry that was the dramatic event. The emphasis was on philosophy and science, on research, on graduate instruction, on the freedom of professors and students (*Lehrfreiheit* and *Lernfreiheit*). The department was created, and the institute. The professor was established as a great figure within and without the university. The Berlin plan spread rapidly throughout Germany, which was then entering a period of industrialization and intense nationalism following the shock of the defeat at the hands of Napoleon. The university carried with it two great new forces: science and nationalism. It is true that the German university system later bogged down through its uncritical reliance on the great professorial figure who ruled for life over his department and institute, and that it could be subverted by Hitler because of its total dependence on the state. But this does not vitiate the fact that the German university in the nineteenth century was one of the vigorous new institutions in the world.

In 1809 when Berlin was founded, the United

States already had a number of colleges developed
on the model of the colleges at Oxford and Cambridge. They concentrated on Calvinism for the
would-be preacher and classics for the young gentleman. Benjamin Franklin had had other ideas for
the University of Pennsylvania, then the College
of Philadelphia, in the 1750's.[6] Reflecting Locke,
he wanted "a *more useful* culture of young minds."
He was interested in training people for agriculture
and commerce; in exploring science. Education
should "serve mankind." These ideas were not to
take root for another century. Drawing on the
French Enlightenment, Jefferson started the University of Virginia with a broad curriculum including mathematics and science, and with the
electives that Eliot was to make so famous at
Harvard half a century later. He put great emphasis on a library—an almost revolutionary idea
at the time. Again the application of the ideas was
to be long delayed.

The real line of development for the modern
American university began with Professor George
Ticknor at Harvard in 1825. He tried to reform
Harvard on the model of Göttingen where he had
studied, and found that reforming Harvard must
wait for an Eliot with forty years and the powers of
the presidency at his disposal. Yale at the time was
the great center of reaction—its famous faculty
report of 1828 was a ringing proclamation to do
nothing, or at least nothing that had not always

been done at Yale or by God.[7] Francis Wayland at
Brown in the 1850's made a great fight for the
German system, including a program of electives,
as did Henry Tappan at Michigan—both without
success.

Then the breakthrough came. Daniel Coit Gilman, disenchanted with the then grim prospects at
California, became the first president of the new
university of Johns Hopkins in 1876. The institution began as a graduate school with an emphasis
ón research. For Flexner, Gilman was the great
hero-figure—and Johns Hopkins "the most stimu-
lating influence that higher education in America
had ever known." Charles W. Eliot at Harvard
followed the Gilman breakthrough and Harvard
during his period (1869 to 1909) placed great emphasis on the graduate school, the professional
school, and research—it became a university. But
Eliot made his own particular contribution by
establishing the elective system permitting students
to choose their own courses of study. Others quickly
followed—Andrew Dickson White at Cornell, James
B. Angell at Michigan, Frederick Barnard at Columbia, William W. Folwell at Minnesota, David
Starr Jordan at Stanford, William Rainey Harper
at Chicago, Charles K. Adams at Wisconsin, Benjamin Ide Wheeler at California. The state universities, just then expanding, followed the Hopkins
idea. Yale and Princeton trailed behind.

The Hopkins idea brought with it the graduate

school with exceptionally high academic standards in what was still a rather new and raw civilization; the renovation of professional education, particularly in medicine; the establishment of the preeminent influence of the department; the creation of research institutes and centers, of university presses and learned journals and the "academic ladder"; and also the great proliferation of courses. If students were to be free to choose their courses (one aspect of the *Lernfreiheit* of the early nineteenth-century German university), then professors were free to offer their wares (as *Lehrfreiheit*, the other great slogan of the developing German universities of a century and a half ago, essentially assured). The elective system, however, came more to serve the professors than the students for whom it was first intended, for it meant that the curriculum was no longer controlled by educational policy as the Yale faculty in 1828 had insisted that it should be. Each professor had his own interests, each professor wanted the status of having his own special course, each professor got his own course—and university catalogues came to include 3,000 or more of them. There was, of course, as a result of the new research, more knowledge to spread over the 3,000 courses; otherwise the situation would have been impossible. In any event, freedom for the student to choose became freedom for the professor to invent; and the professor's love of specialization has become the students' hate of fragmentation. A kind of bizarre version of academic laissez-faire has emerged. The student, unlike Adam Smith's idealized buyer, *must* consume—usually at the rate of fifteen hours a week. The modern university was born.

Along with the Hopkins experiment came the land grant movement—and these two influences turned out to be more compatible than might at first appear. The one was Prussian, the other American; one elitist, the other democratic; one academically pure, the other sullied by contact with the soil and the machine. The one looked to Kant and Hegel, the other to Franklin, Jefferson, and Lincoln. But they both served an industrializing nation and they both did it through research and the training of technical competence. Two strands of history were woven together in the modern American university. Michigan became a German-style university and Harvard a land grant type of institution, without the land.

The land grant movement brought schools of agriculture and engineering (in Germany relegated to the *Technische Hochschulen*), of home economics and business administration; opened the doors of universities to the children of farmers and workers, as well as of the middle and upper classes; introduced agricultural experiment stations and service bureaus. Allan Nevins in commenting on the Morrill Act of 1862 said: "The law annexed wide neglected areas to the domain of instruction. Widening the gates of opportunity, it made democracy freer, more adaptable and more kinetic."[8]

A major new departure in the land grant movement came before World War I when the land grant universities extended their activities beyond their campus boundaries. "The Wisconsin Idea" came to flower under the progressivism of the first Roosevelt and the first La Follette. The University of Wisconsin, particularly during the presidency of Charles Van Hise (1903 to 1918), entered the legislative halls in Madison with reform programs, supported the trade union movement through John R. Commons, developed agricultural and urban extension as never before. The university served the whole state. Other state universities did likewise. Even private universities, like Chicago and Columbia, developed important extension programs.

New contacts with the community were created. University athletics became, particularly in the 1920's, a form of public entertainment, which is not unknown even in the 1960's, even in the Ivy League. Once started, university spectator sports could not be killed even by the worst of teams or the best of de-emphasis; and few universities seriously sought after either.

A counterrevolution against these developments was occasionally waged. A. Lawrence Lowell at Harvard (1909 to 1934) emphasized the undergraduate houses and concentration of course work, as against the graduate work and electives of Eliot. It is a commentary not just on Harvard but also on the modern American university that Eliot and Lowell could look in opposite directions and the same institution could follow them both and glory in it. Universities have a unique capacity for riding off in all directions and still staying in the same place, as Harvard has so decisively demonstrated. At Chicago, long after Lowell, Robert M. Hutchins tried to take the university back to Cardinal Newman, to Thomas Aquinas, and to Plato and Aristotle. He succeeded in reviving the philosophic dialogue he loves so well and practices so expertly; but Chicago went on being a modern American university.

Out of the counterreformation, however, came a great new emphasis on student life—particularly undergraduate. Earnest attempts were made to create American counterparts of Oxford and Cambridge; residence halls, student unions, intramural playfields, undergraduate libraries, counseling centers sprang up in many places during the thirties, forties, and fifties. This was a long way from the pure German model, which had provided the student with only the professor and the classroom, and which had led Tappan to abolish dormitories at Michigan. British influence was back, as it was also with the introduction of honors programs, tutorials, independent study.

Out of all these fragments, experiments, and conflicts a kind of unlikely consensus has been reached.

Undergraduate life seeks to follow the British, who have done the best with it, and an historical line that goes back to Plato; the humanists often find their sympathies here. Graduate life and research follow the Germans, who once did best with them, and an historical line that goes back to Pythagoras; the scientists lend their support to all this. The "lesser" professions (lesser than law and medicine) and the service activities follow the American pattern, since the Americans have been best at them, and an historical line that goes back to the Sophists; the social scientists are most likely to be sympathetic. Lowell found his greatest interest in the first, Eliot in the second, and James Bryant Conant (1934 to 1954) in the third line of development and in the synthesis. The resulting combination does not seem plausible but it has given America a remarkably effective educational institution. A university anywhere can aim no higher than to be as British as possible for the sake of the undergraduates, as German as possible for the sake of the graduates and the research personnel, as American as possible for the sake of the public at large—and as confused as possible for the sake of the preservation of the whole uneasy balance.

THE GOVERNANCE OF THE MULTIVERSITY

The multiversity is an inconsistent institution. It is not one community but several—the community of the undergraduate and the community of the graduate; the community of the humanist, the community of the social scientist, and the community of the scientist; the communities of the professional schools; the community of all the nonacademic personnel; the community of the administrators. Its edges are fuzzy—it reaches out to alumni, legislators, farmers, businessmen, who are all related to one or more of these internal communities. As an institution, it looks far into the past and far into the future, and is often at odds with the present. It serves society almost slavishly—a society it also criticizes, sometimes unmercifully. Devoted to equality of opportunity, it is itself a class society. A community, like the medieval communities of masters and students, should have common interests; in the multiversity, they are quite varied, even conflicting. A community should have a soul, a single animating principle; the multiversity has several—some of them quite good, although there is much debate on which souls really deserve salvation.

The multiversity is a name. This means a great deal more than it sounds as though it might. The name of the institution stands for a certain standard of performance, a certain degree of respect, a certain historical legacy, a characteristic quality of spirit. This is of the utmost importance to faculty and to students, to the government agencies and the industries with which the institution deals. Protection and enhancement of the prestige of the name are central to the multiversity. How good is its reputation, what John J. Corson calls its "institutional character"?[9]

Flexner thought of a university as an "organism." In an organism, the parts and the whole are inextricably bound together. Not so the multiversity—many parts can be added and subtracted with little effect on the whole or even little notice taken or any blood spilled. It is more a mechanism—a series of processes producing a series of results—a mechanism held together by administrative rules and powered by money.

Hutchins once described the modern university as a series of separate schools and departments held together by a central heating system. In an area where heating is less important and the automobile more, I have sometimes thought of it as a series of individual faculty entrepreneurs held together by a common grievance over parking.

It is, also, a system of government like a city, or a city state: the city state of the multiversity. It may be inconsistent but it must be governed—not as the guild it once was, but as a complex entity with greatly fractionalized power. There are several competitors for this power.

The students. The students had all the power once; that was in Bologna. Their guilds ran the university and dominated the masters. And the students were tougher on the masters than the masters have ever been on the students. The Bologna pattern had an impact on Salamanca ánd Spain generally and then in Latin America, where students to this day are usually found in the top governing councils. Their impact is generally more to lower than to raise academic standards although there are exceptions such as Buenos Aires after Peron under the leadership of Risieri Frondizi. Students also involve the university as an institution in the national political controversies of the moment.

Jefferson tried a system of student self-government in the 1820's but quickly abandoned it when all the professors tendered their resignations. He favored self-government by both students and faculty, but never discovered how both could have it at the same time—nor has anybody else. Although José Ortega y Gassett, in addressing the student federation at the University of Madrid, was willing to turn over the entire "mission of the university" to the students, he neglected to comment on faculty reaction.[10]

As part of the "Wisconsin idea" before World War I, there was quite a wave of creation of student governments. They found their power in the area of extracurricular activities, where it has remained. Their extracurricular programs helped broaden student life in such diverse fields as debating, theatrical productions, literary magazines.

Students do have considerable strictly academic influence, however, quite beyond that with which they are usually credited. The system of electives gives them a chance to help determine in which areas and disciplines a university will grow. Their choices, as consumers, guide university expansion and contraction, and this process is far superior to a more rigid guild system of producer determination as in medicine where quotas are traditional. Also students, by their patronage, designate the university teachers. The faculty may, in fact, appoint the faculty, but within this faculty group the students choose the real teachers. In a large university a quarter of the faculty may be selected by the students to do half or more of the actual teaching; the students also "select" ten percent or more to do almost none at all.

The faculty. The guilds of masters organized and ran the University of Paris, and later they did the same at Oxford and Cambridge. Faculty control at Oxford and Cambridge, through the colleges, has remained stronger than anywhere else over the centuries, but even there it has been greatly diminished in recent times.

In the United States, the first great grant of power to the faculty of a major university was at Yale when Jeremiah Day was president (1817 to 1846). It was during the Day regime that the Yale faculty report of 1828 was issued. Harvard has had, by contrast, as McGeorge Bundy has said in his inimitable style, "a tradition of quite high-handed and centralized executive behavior—and it has not suffered, in balance, as a consequence."[11]

Faculties generally in the United States and the

British Commonwealth, some earlier and some later, have achieved authority over admissions, approval of courses, examinations, and granting of degrees— all handled in a rather routine fashion from the point of view of the faculty as a whole. They have also achieved considerable influence over faculty appointments and academic freedom, which are not handled routinely. Faculty control and influence in these areas are essential to the proper conduct of academic life. Once the elective system was established, educational policy became less important to the faculty, although, as at Harvard under Lowell, the elective system was modified to call for general rules on concentration and distribution of work. Since Harvard adopted its program for general education in 1945[12] and Hutchins left Chicago, there has been remarkably little faculty discussion of general educational policy. By contrast, there has been a great deal in England, particularly in the "new universities," where faculty discussion of educational policy has been very lively, and faculty influence, as a consequence, substantial.

Organized faculty control or influence over the general direction of growth of the American multiversity has been quite small, as illustrated by the development of the federal grant university. Individual faculty influence, however, has been quite substantial, even determinative, in the expanding areas of institutes and research grants. Still it is a long way from Paris at the time of Abelard.

Public authority. "Public" authority is a very mixed entity of emperors and popes, ministers of education, grants committees, trustees, and Royal Commissions. But almost everywhere, regardless of the origin of the system, there has come to be a public authority. Even in the Middle Ages, emperors and popes, dukes, cardinals, and city councils came to authorize or establish the universities to make them legitimate—the guild alone was not enough. When Henry VIII had trouble about a wife it shook Oxford and Cambridge to the core.

In modern times, Napoleon was the first to seize control of a university system. He completely reorganized it and made it part of the nationally administered educational system of France, as it remains to this day. He separated off research activities and special training institutions for teachers, engineers, and so forth. The universities became a series of loosely related professional schools. Not until the 1890's were the universities brought back together as meaningful entities and a measure of faculty control restored. Soviet Russia has followed the French pattern with even greater state control.

In Germany, the state governments traditionally have controlled the universities in great detail. So also has the government in Italy. In Latin America a degree of formal autonomy from the government has either been retained or attained, although informal reality usually contradicts the theory.

Even in Great Britain, the "public" has moved in on the faculties. Royal Commissions have helped modernize Oxford and Cambridge. The Redbrick and Scottish universities and London either have had from the beginning or acquired governing boards of a mixed nature, including lay members representative of public authority. Since 1919, and particularly since World War II, the University Grants Committee has made its influence felt in a less and less gentle and more and more effective way.

The lay board has been the distinctive American device for "public" authority in connection with universities, although the device was used in Holland in the late sixteenth century. Beyond the lay board in the state universities are the state department of finance and the governor and the legislature with a tendency toward increasingly detailed review.

Richard Hofstadter has made the interesting observation that the first lay board and the first effective concept of academic freedom developed in Holland at the same time; and that academic freedom has never been inherited from some Golden Age of the past but has instead been imported from the institutions of the surrounding society.[13]

Through all these devices, public influences have been asserted in university affairs. Public influence has increased as much in Paris as student influence has declined in Bologna. Everywhere, with the decreasing exception of Oxford and Cambridge, the ultimate authority lies in the "public" domain; everywhere, with a few exceptions, it is fortunately not exercised in an ultimate fashion. We have, however, come a long way from the guilds of masters, the guilds of students, the guilds of masters and students. The location of power has generally moved from inside to outside the original community of masters and students. The nature of the multiversity makes it inevitable that this historical transfer will not be reversed in any significant fashion, although the multiversity does permit the growth of sub-cultures which can be relatively autonomous and can have an impact on the totality.

The distribution of power is of great importance. In Germany it came to be lodged too completely in the figure of the full professor at one end and the minister of education at the other; in Oxford and Cambridge, at one time, in an oligarchy of professors; in the United States, during a substantial period, almost exclusively in the president; in Latin America, too often, in the students within and the politicians without.

Influences—external and semi-external. Beyond the formal structure of power, as lodged in students, faculty, administration, or "public" instrumentalities, lie the sources of informal influence. The American system is particularly sensitive to the pressures of its many particular publics. Continental and British universities are less intertwined with their surrounding societies than the American and thus more inward-looking and self-contained. When "the borders of the campus are the boundaries of our state," the lines dividing what is internal from what is external become quite blurred; taking the campus to the state brings the state to the campus. In the so-called "private" universities, alumni, donors, foundations, the federal agencies, the professional and business communities bulk large among the semi-external influences; and in the so-called "public" universities, the agricultural, trade union, and public school communities are likely to be added to the list, and also a more searching press. The multiversity has many "publics" with many interests; and by the very nature of the multiversity many of these interests are quite legitimate and others are quite frivolous.

The administration. The original medieval universities had at the start nothing that could be identified as a separate administration, but one quickly developed. The guild of masters or students selected a rector; and later there were deans of the faculties. At Oxford and Cambridge, there came to be the masters of the colleges. In more modern times in France, Germany, and Italy, the rector has come to stand between the faculty and the minister of education, closer to the minister of education in France and closer to the faculty in Germany; internally he has served principally as chairman of the council of deans where deans still retain substantial authority as in France and Italy. In Germany the full professor, chairman of his department, director of his institute, is a figure of commanding authority.

Even in England, even in Oxford and Cambridge, the central administration is attaining more influence—the vice chancellorship can no longer be rotated casually among the masters. The vice chancellor now must deal with the university grants committee and the vice chancellors of the other universities. The university itself is a much more important unit with its research laboratories, central library, its lecturers in specialized subjects; the college is much less self-contained than it was. All of this has created something of a crisis in the administration of Oxford and Cambridge where administrators once were not to be seen or heard and the work was accomplished by a handful of clerks working in a Dickensian office. Oxbridge is becoming more like the Redbricks. London is *sui generis*.

The general rule is that the administration everywhere becomes, by force of circumstances if not by choice, a more prominent feature of the university. As the institution becomes larger, administration becomes more formalized and separated as a distinct function; as the institution becomes more complex, the role of administration becomes more central in integrating it; as it becomes more related to the once external world, the administration assumes the burdens of these relationships. The managerial revolution has been going on also in the university.

MULTIVERSITY PRESIDENT, GIANT
OR MEDIATOR-INITIATOR?

It is sometimes said that the American multiversity president is a two-faced character. This is not
so. If he were, he could not survive. He is a many-
faced character, in the sense that he must face in
many directions at once while contriving to turn his
back on no important group. In this he is different in
degree from his counterparts of rectors and vice
chancellors, since they face in fewer directions
because their institutions have fewer doors and
windows to the outside world. The difference,
however, is not one of kind. And intensities of
relationships vary greatly; the rector of a Latin
American university, from this point of view, may
well have the most trying task of all, though he is less
intertwined in a range of relationships than the
North American university president.

The university president in the United States is
expected to be a friend of the students, a colleague
of the faculty, a good fellow with the alumni, a sound
administrator with the trustees, a good speaker with
the public, an astute bargainer with the foundations
and the federal agencies, a politician with the state
legislature, a friend of industry, labor, and agriculture, a persuasive diplomat with donors, a champion
of education generally, a supporter of the profes-

sions (particularly law and medicine), a spokesman to the press, a scholar in his own right, a public servant at the state and national levels, a devotee of opera and football equally, a decent human being, a good husband and father, an active member of a church. Above all he must enjoy traveling in airplanes, eating his meals in public, and attending public ceremonies. No one can be all of these things. Some succeed at being none.

He should be firm, yet gentle; sensitive to others, insensitive to himself; look to the past and the future, yet be firmly planted in the present; both visionary and sound; affable, yet reflective; know the value of a dollar and realize that ideas cannot be bought; inspiring in his visions yet cautious in what he does; a man of principle yet able to make a deal; a man with broad perspective who will follow the details conscientiously; a good American but ready to criticize the status quo fearlessly; a seeker of truth where the truth may not hurt too much; a source of public policy pronouncements when they do not reflect on his own institution. He should sound like a mouse at home and look like a lion abroad. He is one of the marginal men in a democratic society— of whom there are many others—on the margin of many groups, many ideas, many endeavors, many characteristics. He is a marginal man but at the very center of the total process.

Who is he really?

To Flexner, he was a hero-figure, "a daring pioneer" who filled an "impossible post" yet some of his accomplishments were "little short of miraculous"; thus the "forceful president"—the Gilman, the Eliot, the Harper. The necessary revolutions came from on high. There should be Giants in the Groves. To Thorstein Veblen he was a "Captain of Erudition,"[14] and Veblen did not think well of captains. To Upton Sinclair, the university president was "the most universal faker and most variegated prevaricator that has yet appeared in the civilized world."[15]

To the faculty, he is usually not a hero-figure. Hutchins observed that the faculty really "prefer anarchy to any form of government"[16]—particularly the presidential form.

The issue is whether the president should be "leader" or "officeholder," as Hutchins phrased it; "educator" or "caretaker," as Harold W. Dodds[17] stated it; "creator" or "inheritor," as Frederick Rudolph[18] saw it; "initiator" as viewed by James L. Morrill[19] or consensus-seeker as viewed by John D. Millett;[20] the wielder of power or the persuader, as visualized by Henry M. Wriston;[21] "pump" or "bottleneck" as categorized by Eric Ashby.[22]

The case for leadership has been strongly put by Hutchins. A university needs a purpose, "a vision of the end." If it is to have a "vision," the president must identify it; and, without vision, there is "aimlessness" and the "vast chaos of the American university." "The administrator must accept a special responsibility for the discussion, clarification, definition and proclamation of this end." He must be a "troublemaker, for every change in education is a change in the habits of some members of the faculty." For all this he needs the great "moral virtues" of "courage," "fortitude," "justice," and "prudence." In looking for administrators who really thought and wrote about the "end" of their institution, Hutchins particularly identified Marcus Aurelius as the great prototype.[23] Lowell, too, believed a president should have a "plan" and that although the faculty was "entitled to propose changes," the plan should not basically be subject to interference. He also had the rather quaint idea that the president should "never feel hurried" or "work . . . under pressure."[24]

There were such leaders in higher education. Hutchins was one. Lowell was another; and so was Eliot. When Eliot was asked by a faculty member of the medical school how it could be after eighty years of managing its own affairs the faculty had to accommodate to so many changes, he could answer, "There is a new president."[25] Even in Oxford, of all places, as it belatedly adapted to the new world of scholarship, Benjamin Jowett as Master of Balliol could set as his rule: "Never retract, never explain. Get it done and let them howl."[26] Lord Bryce could comment in his *American Commonwealth* on the great authority of the president in the American university, on his "almost monarchical position."[27]

But the day of the monarchs has passed—the day

when Benjamin Ide Wheeler could ride his white horse across the Berkeley campus or Nicholas Murray Butler rule from Morningside Heights. Flexner rather sadly recorded that "the day of the excessively autocratic president is . . . over. He has done a great service . . ." Paul Lazarsfeld could observe the "academic power vacuum" that resulted —leadership no longer taken by the president nor assumed by the faculty, with the result of little "institutional development."[28] Hutchins was the last of the giants in the sense that he was the last of the university presidents who really tried to change his institution and higher education in any fundamental way. Instead of the not always so agreeable autocracy, there is now the usually benevolent bureaucracy, as in so much of the rest of the world. Instead of the Captain of Erudition or even David Riesman's "staff sergeant," there is the Captain of the Bureaucracy who is sometimes a galley slave on his own ship; and "no great revolutionary figure is likely to appear."[29]

The role of giant was never a happy one. Hutchins concluded that the administrator has many ways to lose, and no way to win, and came to acknowledge that patience, which he once called a "delusion and a snare," was also a virtue. "It is one thing to get things done. It is another to make them last." The experience of Tappan at Michigan was typical of many, as Angell later saw it: "Tappan was the largest figure of a man that ever appeared on the Michigan campus. And he was stung to death by gnats."[30]

The giant was seldom popular with the faculty and was often bitterly opposed, as in the "revolution" against Wheeler at California. And faculty government gained strength as faculties gained distinction. The experiences of Tappan, Wheeler, Hutchins, even Thomas Jefferson, are part of the lore of the university presidency. So are those of Wayland, who resigned from Brown in frustration after vainly trying something new, Woodrow Wilson with all his battles over innovations at Princeton, and many others.

Moreover the university has changed; it has become bigger and more complex, more tensed with checks and balances. As Rudolph saw it, there came to be "a delicate balance of interests, a polite tug of war, a blending of emphases." The presidency was "an office fraught with so many perils, shot through with so many ambiguities, an office that was many things to many men."[31] There are more elements to conciliate, fewer in a position to be led. The university has become the multiversity and the nature of the presidency has followed this change.

Also, the times have changed. The giants were innovators during a wave of innovation, to use the terms of Joseph Schumpeter drawn from another context. The American university required vast renovation to meet the needs of the changing and growing nation. As Eliot said in his inaugural address, "The University must accommodate itself promptly to significant changes in the character of the people for whom it exists." The title of Wilson's inaugural address was, "Princeton for the Nation's Service." They and others helped take what had been denominational colleges and turn them into modern national universities. They were not inventors—the Germans did the inventing—but they came along at a stage in history when massive innovation was the order of the day. The giants today, when found at all, are more likely to be in a few of the old Latin American universities undergoing modernization or the new British universities in the midst of an intense discussion of educational policy.

The giants had performed "a great service," but gentler hands were needed. University administration reverted to the more standard British model of "government by consent and after consultation."[32] There is a "kind of lawlessness"[33] in any large university with many separate sources of initiative and power; and the task is to keep this lawlessness within reasonable bounds. The president must seek "consensus" in a situation when there is a "struggle for power" among groups that share it.[34] "The president must use power economically, and persuasion to the fullest extent."[35] As Allan Nevins sees it, "The sharpest strain on growth lies not in finding the teachers, but expert administrators," and the new type of president required by the large universities "will be a coordinator rather than a creative leader . . . an expert executive, a tactful moderator. . . ."[36]

Academic government has taken the form of the Guild, as in the colleges of Oxford and Cambridge until recent times; of the Manor, as in Columbia under Butler; and of the United Nations, as in the modern multiversity. There are several "nations" of students, of faculty, of alumni, of trustees, of public groups. Each has its territory, its jurisdiction, its form of government. Each can declare war on the others; some have the power of veto. Each can settle its own problems by a majority vote, but altogether they form no single constituency. It is a pluralistic society with multiple cultures. Coexistence is more likely than unity. Peace is one priority item, progress another.

The president in the multiversity is leader, educator, creator, initiator, wielder of power, pump; he is *also* officeholder, caretaker, inheritor, consensus-seeker, persuader, bottleneck. But he is mostly a mediator.

The first task of the mediator is peace—how he may "the Two-and-Seventy jarring Sects confute." Peace within the student body, the faculty, the trustees; and peace between and among them. Peace between the "Two Cultures" and the "Three Cultures" and their subcultures; among all the ideas competing for support. Peace between the internal environment of the academic community and the external society that surrounds and sometimes almost engulfs it. But peace has its attributes. There is the "workable compromise" of the day that resolves the current problem. Beyond this lies the effective solution that enhances the long-run distinction and character of the institution. In seeking it, there are some things that should not be compromised, like freedom and quality—then the mediator needs to become the gladiator. The dividing lines between these two roles may not be as clear as crystal, but they are at least as fragile.

The second task is progress; institutional and personal survival are not enough. A multiversity is inherently a conservative institution but with radical functions. There are so many groups with a legitimate interest in the status quo, so many veto groups; yet the university must serve a knowledge explosion and a population explosion simultaneously. The president becomes the central mediator among the values of the past, the prospects for the future, and the realities of the present. He is the mediator among groups and institutions moving at different rates of speed and sometimes in different directions; a carrier of change—as infectious and sometimes as feared as a "Typhoid Mary." He is not an innovator for the sake of innovation, but he must be sensitive to the fruitful innovation. He has no new and bold "vision of the end." He is driven more by necessity than by voices in the air. "Innovation" may be the historical "measurement of success," the great characterizing feature of the "giants of the past";[37] but innovations sometimes succeed best when they have no obvious author. Lowell once observed that a president "cannot both do things and get credit for them"—that he should not "cackle like a hen that laid an egg."

The ends are already given—the preservation of the eternal truths, the creation of new knowledge, the improvement of service wherever truth and knowledge of high order may serve the needs of man. The ends are there; the means must be ever improved in a competitive dynamic environment. There is no single "end" to be discovered; there are several ends and many groups to be served.

The quality of the mediation is subject to judgment on two grounds, the keeping of the peace and the furthering of progress—the resolution of inter-personal and inter-group warfare, and the reconciliation of the tug of the anchor to the past with the pull of the Holy Grail of the future. Unfortunately peace and progress are more frequently enemies than friends; and since, in the long run, progress is more important than peace to a university, the effective mediator must, at times, sacrifice peace to progress. The ultimate test is whether the mediation permits progress to be made fast enough and in the right directions, whether the needed innovations take precedence over the conservatism of the institution. Mediators, though less dramatic than giants, are not a homogenized group; they only look that way.

They also appear to some people to be doing very little of consequence. Yet their role is absolutely essential if carried out constructively. They serve something of the function of the clerk of the meeting for the Quakers—the person who keeps the business moving, draws forth ideas, seeks the "sense of the meeting." David Riesman has suggested the term "evocator." The techniques must be those of the mediator; but to the techniques may also be added the goals of the innovator. The essence of the role, when adequately performed, is perhaps best conveyed by the term "mediator-initiator."

Power is not necessary to the task, though there must be a consciousness of power. The president must police its use by the constituent groups, so that none will have too much or too little or use it too unwisely. To make the multiversity work really effectively, the moderates need to be in control of each power center and there needs to be an attitude of tolerance between and among the power centers, with few territorial ambitions. When the extremists get in control of the students, the faculty, or the trustees with class warfare concepts, then the "delicate balance of interests" becomes an actual war.

The usual axiom is that power should be commensurate with responsibility, but, for the president, the *opportunity to persuade* should be commensurate with the responsibility. He must have ready access to each center of power, a fair chance in each forum of opinion, a chance to paint reality in place of illusion and to argue the cause of reason as he sees it.

Not all presidents seek to be constructive mediators amid their complexities. One famous president of a New York university succeeded in being at home only five months in five years. Some find it more pleasant to attend meetings, visit projects abroad, even give lectures at other universities; and at home they attend ceremonial functions, go to the local clubs, and allow the winds of controversy to swirl past them. Others look for "visions." But most presidents are in the control tower helping the real pilots make their landings without crashes, even in the fog.

Hutchins wrote of the four moral virtues for a university president. I should like to suggest a slightly different three—judgment, courage, and fortitude—but the greatest of these is fortitude since others have so little charity. The mediator, whether in government or industry or labor relations or domestic quarrels, is always subject to some abuse. He wins few clear-cut victories; he must aim more at avoiding the worst than seizing the best. He must find satisfaction in being *equally* distasteful to each of his constituencies; he must reconcile himself to the harsh reality that successes are shrouded in silence while failures are spotlighted in notoriety. The president of the multiversity must be content to hold its constituent elements loosely together and to move the whole enterprise another foot ahead in what often seems an unequal race with history.

LIFE IN THE MULTIVERSITY

The "Idea of a University" was a village with its priests. The "Idea of a Modern University" was a town—a one-industry town—with its intellectual oligarchy. "The Idea of a Multiversity" is a city of infinite variety. Some get lost in the city; some rise to the top within it; most fashion their lives within one of its many subcultures. There is less sense of community than in the village but also less sense of confinement. There is less sense of purpose than within the town but there are more ways to excel. There are also more refuges of anonymity— both for the creative person and the drifter. As against the village and the town, the "city" is more like the totality of civilization as it has evolved and more an integral part of it; and movement to and from the surrounding society has been greatly accelerated. As in a city, there are many separate endeavors under a single rule of law.

The students in the "city" are older, more likely to be married, more vocationally oriented, more drawn from all classes and races than the students in the village;[38] and they find themselves in a most intensely competitive atmosphere. They identify less with the total community and more with its subgroups. Burton R. Clark and Martin Trow have a particularly interesting typology of these subcultures: the "collegiate" of the fraternities and sororities and the athletes and activities majors; the "academic" of the serious students; the "vocational" of the students seeking training for specific jobs; and the "nonconformist" of the political activists, the aggressive intellectuals, and the bohemians.[39] These subcultures are not mutually exclusive, and some of the fascinating pageantry of the multiversity is found in their interaction one on another.

The multiversity is a confusing place for the student. He has problems of establishing his identity and sense of security within it. But it offers him a vast range of choices, enough literally to stagger the mind. In this range of choices he encounters the opportunities and the dilemmas of freedom. The casualty rate is high. The walking wounded are many. *Lernfreiheit*—the freedom of the student to pick and choose, to stay or to move on—is triumphant.

Life has changed also for the faculty member. The multiversity is in the main stream of events. To the teacher and the researcher have been added the consultant and the administrator. Teaching is less central than it once was for most faculty members; research has become more important. This has given rise to what has been called the "nonteacher" [40]—"the higher a man's standing, the less he has to do with students"—and to a threefold

class structure of what used to be "the faculty":
those who only do research, those who only teach
(and they are largely in an auxiliary role), and
those who still do some of both. In one university I
know, the proportions at the Ph.D. level or its
equivalent are roughly one researcher to two teachers to four who do both.

Consulting work and other sources of additional
income have given rise to what is called the "affluent
professor," a category that does include some but
by no means all of the faculty. Additionally, many
faculty members, with their research assistants and
teaching assistants, their departments and institutes,
have become administrators. A professor's life has
become, it is said, "a rat race of business and activity, managing contracts and projects, guiding
teams and assistants, bossing crews of technicians,
making numerous trips, sitting on committees for
government agencies, and engaging in other distrac-
tions necessary to keep the whole frenetic business
from collapse." [41]

The intellectual world has been fractionalized
as interests have become much more diverse; and
there are fewer common topics of conversation at
the faculty clubs. Faculty government has become
more cumbersome, more the avocation of active
minorities; and there are real questions whether it
can work effectively on a large scale, whether it can
agree on more than preservation of the status quo.

Faculty members are less members of the particular university and more colleagues within their national academic discipline groups.

But there are many compensations. "The American professoriate" is no longer, as Flexner once called it, "a proletariat." Salaries and status have risen considerably. The faculty member is more a fully participating member of society, rather than a creature on the periphery; some are at the very center of national and world events. Research opportunities have been enormously increased. The faculty member within the big mechanism and with all his opportunities has a new sense of independence from the domination of the administration or his colleagues; much administration has been effectively decentralized to the level of the individual professor. In particular, he has a choice of roles and mixtures of roles to suit his taste as never before. He need not leave the Groves for the Acropolis unless he wishes; but he can, if he wishes. He may even become, as some have, essentially a professional man with his home office and basic retainer on the campus of the multiversity but with his clients scattered from coast to coast. He can also even remain the professor of old, as many do. There are several patterns of life from which to choose. So the professor too has greater freedom. *Lehrfreiheit*, in the old German sense of the freedom of the professor to do as he pleases, also is triumphant.

What is the justification of the modern American

multiversity? History is one answer. Consistency with the surrounding society is another. Beyond that, it has few peers in the preservation and dissemination and examination of the eternal truths; no living peers in the search for new knowledge; and no peers in all history among institutions of higher learning in serving so many of the segments of an advancing civilization. Inconsistent internally as an institution, it is consistently productive. Torn by change, it has the stability of freedom. Though it has not a single soul to call its own, its members pay their devotions to truth.

The multiversity in America is perhaps best seen at work, adapting and growing, as it responded to the massive impact of federal programs beginning with World War II. A vast transformation has taken place without a revolution, for a time almost without notice being taken. The multiversity has demonstrated how adaptive it can be to new opportunities for creativity; how responsive to money; how eagerly it can play a new and useful role; how fast it can change while pretending that nothing has happened at all; how fast it can neglect some of its ancient virtues. What are the current realities of the federal grant university?

2

THE REALITIES OF THE
FEDERAL GRANT
UNIVERSITY

Two great impacts, beyond all other forces, have molded the modern American university system and made it distinctive. Both impacts have come from sources outside the universities. Both have come primarily from the federal government. Both have come in response to national needs.

The first was the land grant movement. Abraham Lincoln signed the Morrill Act in 1862. This act set the tone for the development of American universities, both public and private, for most of the ensuing hundred years. It was one of the most seminal pieces of legislation ever enacted.

The land grant movement came in response to the rapid industrial and agricultural development of the United States that attained such momentum in the middle of the last century. Universities were to assist this development through training that went beyond the creation of "gentlemen," and of teachers, preachers, lawyers, and doctors; through research related to the technical advance of farming and manufacturing; through service to many and ultimately to almost all of the economic and political segments of society. The land grant movement was also responsive to a growing democratic, even egalitarian and populist, trend in the nation. Pursuing this trend, higher education was to be open to all qualified young people from all walks of life. It was to serve less the perpetuation of an elite class and more the creation of a relatively classless society, with the doors of opportunity open to all through education.

This was a dramatic break with earlier American traditions in higher education. It created a new social force in world history. Nowhere before had universities been so closely linked with the daily life of so much of their societies. The university campus came to be one of the most heavily traveled crossroads in America—an intersection traversed by farmers, businessmen, politicians, students from almost every corner of almost every state. The cloister and the ivory tower were destroyed by being thrown open to all qualified comers.

Supporting the impact of the land grant movement was the effect on American universities of the model supplied by Germany. This German model gave academic respectability and content to the "land grant" idea; and Harvard, a private university with a long academic tradition, could travel much the same path of development as Cornell, a newly established land grant institution. German intellectualism and American populism were merged in the new university. Pure intellect and raw pragmatism made an unlikely but successful alliance.

The second great impact on the universities began with federal support of scientific research during World War II. The wartime laboratories that were the forerunners of such continuing government-financed research centers as the Lincoln Laboratory at the Massachusetts Institute of Technology, the Argonne at Chicago, and the Lawrence Radiation Laboratory at California, opened a new age. The major universities were enlisted in national defense and in scientific and technological development as never before. (In World War I the universities had only been a source of raw recruits.)

Instead of Gilman, Eliot, and White, there were now such new pioneers as Conant, Compton, and Bush to guide this alliance of the federal government with the universities. Don K. Price notes that "in the hands of Vannevar Bush, James B. Conant, and Karl T. Compton the government contract became a new type of federalism."[1] In addition to the industrial revolution there was now the scientific revolution to be served. In addition to the stimulus of Germany, there was Russia—for Russian scientific achievements both before and after Sputnik were an immense spur to the new departure. American universities have been changed almost as much by the federal research grant as by the land grant idea.

It is interesting that American universities, which pride themselves on their autonomy, should have taken their special character as much or more from the pressures of their environment as from their own inner desires; that institutions which identify themselves either as "private" or as "state" should have found their greatest stimulus in federal initiative; that universities which are part of a highly decentralized and varied system of higher education should, nevertheless, have responded with such fidelity and alacrity to national needs; that institutions which had their historical origins in the training of "gentlemen" should have committed themselves so fully to the service of brute technology.

The "federal grant" university has been emerging over the past twenty years, but until recently it has developed more by force of circumstances than by conscious design. The universities most affected have been making largely piecemeal adjustments to the new phenomena without any great effort at an overall view of what has been happening to them. Perhaps this was just as well—the transition probably was smoother precisely because it was not subjected to critical analysis. The federal government and the leading universities entered into a common-law marriage unblessed by predetermined policies and self-surveys—but nonetheless they formed a very productive union.

All this, however, as was inevitable, is being changed. Harvard has now studied itself. So has Princeton. Brookings and Carnegie have studied us all; so have the Department of Health, Education, and Welfare; the President's Science Advisory Committee; the American Council on Education; and the American Assembly.[2] The principal conclusion was predictable: the federal colossus had the power to influence the most ruggedly individual of universities. A paradox emerged: the better and the more individual the university, the greater its chances of succumbing to the federal embrace. Washington did not waste its money on the second-rate.

Soon there will be a national policy as well as nationwide activity, and I am at least a little concerned. All these studies have identified problems that we knew all along to exist. But now that we have publicly identified the problems, we shall be expected to deal with them; and in dealing with them we shall create new problems. Mostly, we shall have to strive for "balance" in a number of different ways. We shall have to "balance" the wishes of individual scholars with those of their institutions; New England with the South; the sciences with the humanities; research with teaching;

graduate training with undergraduate education; merit with politics; the judgment of specialists with general formulae. And yet one of the more productive aspects of federal involvement to date has been its imbalance.

We are clearly entering the second phase of the "federal grant" development. The first I shall identify as the phase of "intuitive imbalance," and the new phase just emerging as one of "bureaucratic balance." It is a good time to examine where we have been and where we may be going. We are in the midst of a vast transformation of university life and none of us can be too sure where we really are going; but we can try to peer ahead.

As a basis for discussing the two phases of federal grant development, I shall briefly review the essential facts about federal involvement with universities in this country.

¶ Federal interest in higher education dates from 1787. That year saw the beginning of endowment of public institutions of higher education with public lands, following the example of the Northwest Ordinance of 1785, which provided land to support public schools at the lower levels. However, this interest was not made effective until the Morrill Land Grant Act of 1862. Then the Second Morrill Act in 1890 supplemented the original land grants with federal grants of funds to support college instruction in specified subjects; these grants still continue, and, in fact, have recently been expanded.

Federal interest in higher education was further made effective by the Hatch Act in 1887, establishing the Agricultural Experiment Stations, and by the Smith-Lever Act in 1914, creating the Agricultural Extension Service. During World War I, the ROTC program was established. During the Great Depression, universities were involved in the programs of the Work Projects Administration and National Youth Administration. During World War II, universities participated heavily in the Engineering, Science and Management War Training Program inaugurated in 1940. In that same year, the National Defense Research Committee (later the Office of Scientific Research and Development) was established, and leading universities became engaged in the various programs of war research which it set up.

After World War II and again after the Korean conflict, the "G.I. Bill" and the corresponding bill for Korean veterans sent a seismic shock through academic life.

Despite this long history of federal interest, however, it is evident that with the exception of the comparatively restricted areas of agriculture and military training, there was no continuing federal involvement with higher education until World War II.

¶ Currently, federal support has become a major factor in the total performance of many universities, and the sums involved are substantial. Higher education in 1960 received about $1.5 billion from the federal government—a hundredfold increase in twenty years. About one third of this $1.5 billion was for university-affiliated research centers; about one third for project research within universities; and about one third for other things, such as residence hall loans, scholarships, and teaching programs. This last third was expended at colleges as well as universities, but the first two thirds almost exclusively at universities, and at relatively few of them.

The $1 billion for research, though only 10 percent of total federal support for research and development, accounted for 75 percent of all university expenditures on research and 15 percent of total university budgets. Clearly the shape and nature of university research are profoundly affected by federal monies.

¶ Federal research funds to universities flow primarily from six agencies. In 1961 the percentage distribution was as follows:

Department of Health, Education, and Welfare .. 39
(37 percent was from National Institutes of Health alone)
Department of Defense 32
National Science Foundation 11
Atomic Energy Commission 8
Department of Agriculture 6
National Aeronautics and Space
    Administration 3
Other agencies 1

(These figures do not include funds for university-operated government research centers.)

This federal support has been almost exclusively identified with three great and somewhat inter-related national concerns: defense (40 percent of the total in 1961, including support by the Department of Defense and the Atomic Energy Commission); scientific and technological progress (20 percent—National Science Foundation, Department of Agriculture, and NASA); and health (37 percent—through the National Institutes of Health). Federal support has not been directed explicitly toward strengthening universities generally, or one or more universities specifically, in any over-all fashion—as might be said of the University Grants Committee in Great Britain.

¶ Federal research expenditures have been largely restricted to the physical and biomedical sciences, and engineering, with only about 3 percent for the social sciences and hardly any support for the humanities.

¶ Among the totality of university functions, federal support has been heavily concentrated on research and on graduate and postdoctoral training in fields of national interest.

¶ The preferred approach of the federal government to the use of university facilities for research has been (a) the specialized research center—by 1963 there were fourteen major ones,[3] and (b) the research project. Projects have been supported for relatively short terms and specific purposes; and support has been awarded, usually on the advice of qualified experts, on the basis of prospective performance.

¶ Federal research expenditures have been heavily focused on a relatively few institutions. If both project research and large research centers are included, six universities received 57 percent of the funds in a recent fiscal year, and twenty universities received 79 percent. If project research alone is considered, the figures are 28 and 54 percent. As a percentage of total university expenditures for all purposes among the leading twenty recipients, federal funds have amounted to 20 to 50 percent when project research alone is counted and from 20 to over 80 percent when the research centers are added. These twenty universities are only about one tenth of all universities in the United States. They constitute the primary federal grant universities.

¶ Recently there has been some spreading out of federal interest from the physical and biomedical to the social sciences; from graduate to undergraduate training; from a selective few to an expanded number of universities.

PHASE ONE: INTUITIVE IMBALANCE

For about twenty years now, Congress has been deciding in which general areas the partnership between the federal government and the universities should be developed. The areas chosen have been defense, scientific and technological progress, and health. Decisions have not been based on thorough study of national priorities. They have been made pragmatically, in response to the felt needs of the nation and of the people in accord with the possibilities of the times, and also, to an extent, in response to the urgings of very powerful lobbies. The atom was split, and could be used for war and peace. The "cold war" followed World War II and necessitated further defense work. Health became a matter of great national concern. Possibilities for space exploration developed. Congress reacted quickly to each of these realities.

Once Congress initiated a program, federal administrative officers turned to those universities best able to give immediate and effective assistance on the individual programs; or rather they turned to those scientists in the best position to respond quickly and efficiently—and those scientists were principally located in a limited number of institutions. These actions were not undertaken on the basis of any general review of institutional capacity or potential capacity, but on quick and ready apprehension of possibilities and response to them. The test was who could most effectively do the job at hand. The process was more intuitive than studied.

For about twenty years, universities have been accepting the research centers and projects as proposed by faculty members and government agencies, making such day-to-day adjustments as were needed and possible. In consequence, these universities have been profoundly affected. The whole process has been one of starting new endeavors, and this has changed the pre-existing "balance" in several ways. Some real and some not so real issues have arisen for the universities.

1. *Federal control and federal influence.* Federal control as a substantive issue is, as Sidney Hook has said, a "red herring."[4] With a few exceptions—the generally necessary exception of secrecy in certain types of work and the unnecessary exception of the disclaimer affidavit required by the National Defense Education Act—there has been no control in any deleterious sense. By way of contrast, state control of state universities has been a real problem.[5] The federal government has customarily put scientifically trained persons in charge of science programs and they have operated fully within academic traditions.

The real problem is not one of federal control but of federal influence. A federal agency offers a project. A university need not accept—but, as a practical matter, it usually does. One of the quickest ways to lose a faculty member is by refusing to accept the grant he has just negotiated with his counterpart in Washington. Out of this reality have followed many of the consequences of federal aid for the universities; and they have been substantial. That they are subtle, slowly cumulative and gentlemanly makes them all the more potent.

2. *University control and the agency as alma mater.* A university's control over its own destiny has been substantially reduced. University funds from tuition and fees, gifts and endowments, and state sources go through the usual budget-making procedures and their assignment is subject to review in accordance with internal policy. Federal research funds, however, are usually negotiated by the individual scholar with the particular agency, and so bypass the usual review process. Thus 20 to 50 to 80 percent of a university's expenditures may be handled outside the normal channels. These funds in turn commit some of the university's own funds; they influence the assignment of space; they determine the distribution of time between teaching and research; to a large extent they establish the areas in which the university grows the fastest. Almost imperceptibly, a university is changed.

The authority of the department chairman, the dean, the president are thereby reduced; so also is the role of faculty government. This may have its advantages. Scholars seem to prefer dealing with their professional counterparts in Washington rather than with their colleagues and administrators at home.[6] Also the university's internal process of distributing funds would be generally less selective and less flexible than the federal research project approach. Within a university, the tendency is to give each faculty member about the same opportunity and once having given it to keep giving it thereafter; but the project method allows more attention to exceptional merit and has the advantage that all projects may end some time. Additionally, federal agencies are more responsive to particular national needs than the universities would be, given the same amount of money to spend according to their own priority system.

There are, however, clearly detrimental effects. Some faculty members come to use the pressure of their agency contacts against their university. They may try to force the establishment of a new administrative unit or the assignment of land for their own special building, in defiance of general university policy or priorities. These pressures, of course, should be withstood; they speak well neither of the professor nor of the agency. Also, some faculty members tend to shift their identification and loyalty from their university to the agency in Washington. Their concern with the general welfare of the university is eroded and they become tenants rather than owners, taking their grants with them as they change their institutional lodgings. The university, as Allen Wallis, president of the University of Rochester, has remarked, becomes to an extent a "hotel." The agency becomes the new alma mater. The research entrepreneur becomes a euphoric schizophrenic.

It has been said that, in the face of federal aid,

university presidents have "abdicated" their responsibilities for the general conduct of their institutions.
I would put it differently—they have let some things
go by that they would have liked to do differently;
but this is often what they do anyway. There are,
however, especially acute problems when the agency
insists on the tie-in sale (if we do this for you, then
you must do that for us) or when it requires frequent
and detailed progress reports. Then the university
really is less than a free agent. It all becomes a kind
of "putting-out" system with the agency taking the
place of the merchant-capitalist of old. Sweat shops
have developed out of such a system in earlier times
and in other industries.

3. *"Scientists Affluent, Humanists Militant."*[7] Federal
research support has added a new dimension to the
eternal class struggles within a university. To
student versus faculty, assistant versus tenure professors, and faculty versus administrators has been
added a new hierarchical point of tension—that
between humanists and scientists. The scientists, by
and large, in the federal grant universities, get
promoted faster, get more space, get more income
through summer employment and consulting, have
more secretaries and assistants, have greater access
to travel funds and expense accounts, and accumu-
late a greater sense of status within and outside the
academic community. Some humanists obviously
resent all this and consider it quite unfair, even

though their own situation has improved, relative to what it used to be.

However, there is still another side to the story. The scientist who gets a series of projects going can become caught in his own apparatus. Graduate students and staff members become dependent upon him. He is committed to project deadlines and periodic contract negotiations. He is enmeshed in a web of obligations and it is very hard to break out. As a result, he often works hard at things he would rather not do—more often than need be true of the humanist.

There is some current tendency for the brightest of graduate students to prefer the sciences to the social sciences and the humanities,[8] and this will have an impact on comparative faculty quality as between fields of study in the years to come. How much of this has been caused by federal aid and how much by the current liveliness of the different fields is not at all clear. My own impression is that the brightest graduate students flock to the areas with the brightest new ideas, regardless of federal aid.

All this is said to have destroyed the "balance" among fields and it is generally concluded that something should be done about it. The balance among fields, however, has never been a static thing. If it were, philosophy, theology, and the classics would still be the dominant areas of study, as they have not been for a long time. Assuming that the balance of 1942, say, was appropriate for 1942, this does not mean it would have been appropriate for 1962. It is not enough to say that the old "balance" has been destroyed. The real question is what should be the proper balance today? It is clear that the flowering of the Renaissance should have affected the "balance" in the sixteenth century. It would seem likely that the splitting of the atom and the deciphering of the genetic code should in their turn affect the balance of the twentieth century. We should expect the most money and the brightest students and the greatest prestige to follow the most exciting new ideas. By and large they have done so, and this is one way of defining the nature of balance. (Economics was exciting in the 1930's; sociology was more exciting in the 1950's.)

The real question, it seems to me, is not one of balance in any historical or monetary sense, but rather what is most appropriate to each field in each period. "All fields are equal, only some are more equal than others." There should be no effort to do the same things in the same amounts for each field. Each should receive support in accordance with its current potentialities, and potentialities vary. There are no timeless priorities.

The academic community has lived with inequities before. Agriculture in the land grant institutions has had eleven-month appointments, low teaching loads, and heavy research subsidies for decades. Law and medicine have reflected within the academic world some of the power and affluence of their professions in the outside world. These are stated as matters of fact, not as ideal situations.

Generally, I think, it is remarkable and commendable that so high a degree of internal equity has thus far been preserved within the academic world in the face of quite chaotic pressures impinging upon it.

4. *The inevitability of concentration.* The project approach almost automatically led to concentration of federal research effort in a relatively few universities. The universities best equipped to undertake the research were also those with the faculty and facilities to provide for the training of Ph.D.'s. It is no coincidence that the six universities with a little more than 25 percent of project funds graduated about 25 percent of the Ph.D.'s; and a similar situation prevails for the top twenty universities. If "only the best will do,"[9] this concentration of effort is inevitable. A different result would have been quite surprising.

This concentration of effort has undoubtedly strengthened the facilities and improved the quality of faculties of universities already in the front rank. It has probably widened the gap between those of the first and those of the second and third ranks. It may, in fact, have actually injured universities of the second and third ranks and some colleges by turning their potential faculty members into research personnel in the front-rank universities. The good are better; the poor may well be worse. And it has greatly accentuated the differences between colleges and universities.

5. *Teaching the graduates versus teaching the undergraduates.* The much-advertised conflict between teaching and research puts the problem the wrong way. The teaching of graduate students is so closely tied to research that if research is improved, graduate instruction is almost bound to be improved also. And the almost universal experience seems to be that federal research support has improved graduate instruction. There have been better facilities, more research assistantships and fellowships, more research projects in which students can work directly with faculty members—all resulting from federal funds. At the graduate level, there has been a clear gain, and fortunately so, because graduate enrollments at the federal grant universities have been increasing rapidly.

At the undergraduate level, however, the "subtle discounting of the teaching process"[10] has been aided and abetted. Harold Orlans, who conducted the excellent Brookings study of federal aid to universities, concludes that federal research aid "has accelerated the long-standing depreciation of undergraduate education at large universities."[11] This is my own observation, with one exception—that a very few private institutions with long traditions of very high-quality undergraduate instruction have been able to maintain their standards; and this is to their great credit.

The reasons for the general deterioration of undergraduate teaching are several. Teaching loads and student contact hours have been reduced. Faculty members are more frequently on leave or temporarily away from the campus; some are never more than temporarily on campus. More of the instruction falls to teachers who are not members of the regular faculty. The best graduate students prefer fellowships and research assistantships to teaching assistantships. Postdoctoral fellows who might fill the gap usually do not teach. Average class size has been increasing.

There seems to be a "point of no return" after which research, consulting, graduate instruction become so absorbing that faculty efforts can no longer be concentrated on undergraduate instruction as they once were. This process has been going on for a long time; federal research funds have intensified it. As a consequence, undergraduate education in the large university is more likely to be acceptable than outstanding; educational policy from the undergraduate point of view is largely neglected. How to escape the cruel paradox that a superior faculty results in an inferior concern for undergraduate teaching is one of our more pressing problems.

6. *The faculty and the un-faculty.* University scholars

traditionally have both taught and conducted research. But now some scholars are added to the staff in exclusively research capacities—and increasingly with titles suggesting professorial status. They have no teaching responsibilities and are not as yet fully accepted members of the academic community. They usually are not members of the Academic Senate and they usually are not given tenure—both traditional marks of faculty status. In many institutions, however, they may use the name of the university in getting projects under their own direction.

In a far less anomalous position is the faculty member who works on a federally sponsored project during the summer months and part-time during the regular year, and receives much of his pay from the project rather than from the university. But to what extent is he really a university employee and what security of employment does he really have? Obviously, it is no longer so clear as it once was just who is the faculty.

There has been an almost frantic remaking of the rules—new titles created, new relationships established, new classes of citizenship formulated and only partially assimilated. The Harvard catalogue now lists more than 5,000 "Officers of Instruction and Administration," many of whom are not faculty in the traditional sense. The "faculty" in our universities becomes an ever-changing group as the definitions change. If there can still be said to be a "faculty" at all, it is most certainly a different composite than before. Much of the teaching, much of the research are done by the "un-faculty."

7. *University "aid" to the federal government.* Federal aid has been of great benefit to the universities. It has not, however, been without its costs in money and effort. Overhead allowances vary greatly from agency to agency but seldom cover all the indirect as well as the direct costs of sponsored research. Also, matching grants for construction may force a university to upset its own priority system in order to get federal funds. This, of course, is the intent.

Additionally, federal funds have placed great new administrative burdens on the universities—on faculty members, on department chairmen, on deans, on presidents. New classes of administrators have been created—the contracting officer and the research project manager. Administration becomes a much larger aspect of the total university enterprise. Julius A. Stratton has observed, "There is a basic incompatibility between the true spirit of a university and those elements of management which tend to creep into the organization of projects, the planning of programs, and the utilization of costly facilities."[12]

8. *On the borders of temptation.* Immense sums of money have been poured into the universities by the federal government, and universities are highly atomistic entities. The university has the responsibility for but usually not the actual control of these

funds. Some abuses have inevitably developed. Funds have been diverted at times from one use to another—and the other use one not intended by the federal agency. Some faculty members make informal alliances—if you consult on my project, then I should consult on yours—and total income has been pyramided through this exchange of consultancies to occasionally astounding levels. When these same faculty members sit on the federal panels that make the grants, the whole process becomes quite involved, to say the least. Excessive amounts of expensive equipment have at times been purchased, and equipment salesmen chase grants around. Some universities promise not only a base salary but substantial supplemental personal income and allowances from federal grants as a recruiting device in a wilder and wilder upward spiral.

There have been some scandals. There will be more. The federal agencies will exercise increasingly specific controls and the universities dependent on this new standard of living will accept these controls. The universities themselves will have to exercise more stringent controls by centralizing authority, particularly through the audit process. In a few situations, self-restraint has not been enough restraint; as one result, greater external restraint will be imposed in most situations.

With all its problems, however, federal research aid to universities has helped greatly in meeting national needs. It has greatly assisted the universities themselves. The nation is stronger. The leading universities are stronger. As Nathan Pusey reported the unanimous views of the presidents of universities participating in the Carnegie study, federal aid, over all, has been a "good thing."[13] In their turn, the federal grant universities have adapted to their new role quite quickly and effectively.

Professor Don Price has made reference to the following limerick:

> There was a young lady from Kent
> Who said that she knew what it meant
> When men took her to dine,
> Gave her cocktails and wine;
> She knew what it meant—but she went.[14]

I am not so sure that the universities and their presidents always knew what it meant; but one thing is certain—they went.

PHASE TWO: BUREAUCRATIC BALANCE

The general policy of federal agencies in allocating research grants to universities for the last two decades has been one of "seeking excellence wherever it is," one of accepting the established pattern and following it. The new approach is to take more of an over-all view; to change the pattern to a degree. Balance is the new virtue; imbalance the old sin.

The charge, made by Logan Wilson among others, has been that "There is no federal program

—merely programs."[15] The response—in the proposed "National Education Improvement Act of
1963," for example—is to provide: "A comprehen-
sive program of Federal aid to meet selected and
urgent needs of American education on all levels
from elementary school through graduate education; to promote educational quality, expand opportunity for education, and to increase the capacity
of our educational institutions; to provide for the
Nation's needs in skilled manpower, national
growth, and national security."

The new balance calls for developing a larger
number of outstanding centers of graduate instruction and research. The Seaborg report suggested an
expansion from the present fifteen or twenty centers
to thirty or forty over a fifteen-year period.[16] The
National Education Improvement Act envisages
expansion from twenty to seventy. This demand for
geographical dispersion of centers of strength follows, in part, the new realization of the role of a
university as a factor influencing the location of
industry. The Roswell L. Gilpatric report for the
Department of Defense explained the concentration
of defense contracts in California and Massachusetts
by the concentration of research and development
projects in these two states, which in turn was
attributed to the availability of university centers of
substantial strength.[17] An educational and political
effort of considerable dimensions now seeks to re-

order the current pattern of distribution in the name of balance.

Under the National Defense Education Act of 1958, preference is already given to assisting *new* graduate programs in selected subject matter areas. Teaching is being emphasized along with research. Summer refresher courses for teachers of science, improvement of science textbooks, and language laboratories are programs already well established. The National Science Foundation has a large effort under way to improve and renovate equipment for undergraduate teaching in the physical sciences. Undergraduates, as well as graduate students, are being assisted by loans and scholarships. The social sciences are receiving increasing sums of money. More funds are being granted to colleges as well as to universities, and to universities of all ranks. In particular, "institutional grants," to supplement project grants, are being given by the National Science Foundation and the National Institutes of Health. And NASA, among others, makes "training" grants to institutions instead of awarding fellowships to students who may then go wherever they wish. Thus, efforts to achieve greater "balance" are already well under way.

The approach to a university "as an institution" is of particular interest. If additional universities are to be selected to become centers of strength in research and graduate instruction, then it will be necessary for the federal government to be concerned with the "general health of the institution." This will be a notable departure from historical practice, except in agriculture. The Land Grant Association, in commenting on recent recommendations by the President's Science Advisory Committee for dispersion through assistance to institutions as such, said: "The recommendations represent a return to the principles of government-institution relations laid down in the basic land grant legislation, in which the responsibility for internal administration, fiscal management, and proper direction is vested with university officers rather than with agency staffs."[18] It should be noted that *every* state has at least one land grant institution receiving federal support on a formula basis. The parallel with agriculture is not entirely apt, however, since agriculture by its very nature is locally and regionally oriented, but national defense and space exploration are not.

If we are to move toward federal orientation to the "total function of the university," then the University Grants Committee in Great Britain is the outstanding precedent, and one that has received some support in the United States.[19] However, there are only about thirty universities in Great Britain and it is clear what is and what is not a university. Additionally, the University Grants Committee has come to exercise more influence over the establishment of new programs, the cost and size and even the appearance of new buildings, the equalization of faculty salaries among institutions, and the determination of admission policies than would currently be acceptable if it came from the federal government in this country.

Some hard choices must be faced. The decentralized project approach of the last two decades has much to recommend it. It is selective on merit, flexible in accordance with quality of performance, and responsive to national goals. The universities and their scholars retain substantial freedom. But such dominant reliance on the project approach is no longer likely. In fact, the project is already less the chosen instrument than it once was. Productive anarchy is no longer such a politically viable solution.

It is said that support to institutions as such will "give a university the necessary autonomy," and will permit dispersion of effort and better balance in several directions. It is not clear, however, how the particular institutions will be chosen, or, once chosen, how support might subsequently be withdrawn if performance should prove inadequate. It is difficult to assess the merit of a total institution as complex as a modern university. One alternative is to rely on a formula, as in the case of agriculture in the land grant institutions. Another is to be guided by political influence; and this is increasingly happening.

It is reported that Congress already senses its loss

of control to the professional personnel in the various agencies and would like to regain it. "Congress knows it has forfeited much power over science to the Executive and it does not like it."[20] The Harvard self-study report notes the danger of political interference and "log-rolling" inherent in block grants.[21] Inter-university competition would be taken from the quasi-academic arena of the agency committee to the legislative halls.

Additionally, the selection of designated "centers of strength" assumes a single source of designation —a single over-all federal agency or committee. A single agency means a single source of control, as against the current pluralistic situation of several agencies and several sources of influence, with opportunity to pick and choose among them. A single source of control would turn an influential relationship into a really "perilous partnership."[22] Finally, will funds necessarily be better spent for the national interest under institutional control than through the agencies, where decisions are freer from internal rigidities and egalitarian tendencies?

In the battle over institutional versus project support, Congressmen are more likely to prefer the institutional approach than are the professionals in the agencies; the presidents of universities than the researchers within the universities; the less well-established universities than the well-established ones; the humanists than the scientists—generally, those who have less under the project system than those who have more.

It is almost obligatory in educational circles these days to support "excellence" *and* "balance." They are the two magic words. Yet "excellence" and "balance" sometimes pull in different directions. It is also quite necessary to favor "institutional integrity" and to be against "federal control." Yet the institutional grants that aid what we are supposed to favor (integrity) may also aid what we are supposed to be against (control). Turning "integrity" over to the university president may also turn "control" over to the federal government.

How can we really best secure "aristocracy of achievement arising out of democracy of opportunity?"[23]

SOME SUGGESTIONS

The nation does face some grave problems in the field of education. Vastly increased numbers of students are pouring into our schools. Many qualitative deficiencies exist. State and local subdivisions are caught with relatively fixed tax structures, and private endowments and gifts have their limits also. Federal support is the most obvious way out. But federal expenditures themselves are not unlimited, and there are some realistic barriers to certain types of federal involvement.

The first consideration is that the federal government need not and cannot do everything. It seems to me that the educational system of America, good as it generally is, is in the most trouble —and thus in the greatest need of federal help—at the bottom and at the top.

At the bottom is the problem of "drop-outs" from school and "drop-outs" of the unskilled from the employed labor force. Through occupational training and retraining, through counseling, guidance, and relocation, these "drop-outs" should be assisted to acquire skills valuable in a dynamic economy where skill levels are rising at perhaps the fastest rate in history. Full employment is the necessary complement to make such training effective.

At the top, the nation needs more research activity in a number of fields and more personnel of high skill—particularly engineers, scientists, mathematicians, teachers, and medical doctors. A recent Bureau of Labor Statistics survey shows that from now to 1970 the expected supply of engineers and scientists will fill only three quarters of the demand. This leaves a very large gap. The prospect is particularly critical for engineers.

Fortunately the levels where federal aid is most necessary are levels where it is most politically feasible. My suggestions will be limited to higher education, and to the university level in particular.

1. Federal research centers, whenever possible, should be located near and identified with a univer-

sity. A university, with its libraries, colleagues to talk to, and graduate students to train, provides a uniquely favorable environment for such centers. In turn, such centers provide additional research opportunities for the university's faculty members and graduate students. Instead of establishing a research center in isolation and then, perhaps, having to build a new university at the same site, it seems to me best to put the center near some university— even if it doesn't happen to be our own.

2. The project system should be continued in essentially its present form as the major means of supporting the research and graduate instruction programs of universities as well as accomplishing the specific research purposes of the federal government. If project funds double or triple during the decade of the sixties, as now seems likely, it will be possible and necessary to extend more of them beyond the twenty institutions that constitute the primary group of federal grant universities at the present time. Orlans has identified about ten universities, mostly "public" ones, which already deserve considerably more project support on the basis of their existing Ph.D. programs.[24] Other universities will soon be moving into this group in the natural course of events. The project system follows established lines of contact through disciplines and avoids the problems of establishing a new reliance on institutional lines of contact.

The project system has resulted in a "highly

successful working relationship between the government's need for long- and short-term research and the academic scientist's abilities and interests."[25]

To the extent that institutional grants are given, they should follow the project grants. Charles V. Kidd has suggested that 25 percent might be given as free funds to institutions, as against 75 percent in project funds.[26] Twenty-five percent appears to be an adequate figure. These institutional grants could best be used by the universities for new projects, small projects, support of young faculty members unknown in Washington, and of fields neglected in direct federal grants—all on a very flexible basis. Thus the universities' rather different evaluation of "merit" could supplement the standards for merit of the federal agencies. I would hope that the institutional grants would be assigned automatically by the agencies as some percentage of the project grants which are themselves assigned on merit. If "quality must come first,"[27] this is the best way to assure it.

Alvin M. Weinberg has recently made the interesting suggestion that the panel system of reviewing research proposals could be improved as an instrument for making scientific judgments by including on the panels representatives of related fields, as well as representatives of the field in question. "I should think that advice from panels so constituted," he says, "would be tempered by concern for larger issues; in particular the support of a proposed research project would be viewed from the larger perspective of the relevance of that research to the rest of science."[28] The greater impartiality of the panels would also be assured.

Contract and grant overhead should cover reasonable indirect as well as all direct costs.

Federal project funds are increasingly being used to bid salaries and allowances up and to bid teaching assignments down. How much further such competition can go without raising grave policy problems for the federal agencies is problematical. The market is sufficiently active without this added inflationary stimulus; and the universities are sufficiently in trouble with internal inequities and reduction of teaching time.

There is currently arising a three-sided competitive struggle for research and development work, involving industry, the universities, and the government itself.[29] The universities should be preferred for basic research and for such other research as is readily related to graduate instruction.

It is being suggested, and also being implemented, that federal grants and contracts be channeled increasingly into liberal arts colleges to assist faculty research and the training of outstanding undergraduate students. This process can easily subvert the colleges from their primary obligation and start them on the way to becoming quite different types of institutions. With a project-by-project approach this is almost bound to happen. Would it not be well for the governing bodies of such colleges to examine the implications of this changed role before the process of project-by-project transformation of the nature of the institution is begun? If they accept the role they should accept it by a conscious policy decision.

3. To aid the teaching function of universities during the "deficit years" of greatly swollen enrollments just ahead, federal agencies should permit, even encourage, postdoctoral fellows and research professors to teach one-quarter or even one-third time at no cost to the institution. The present system increases the size of the "un-faculty" and widens the gap between the researcher and the student. Also, the further creation of research career professorships might well be examined. Are they really necessary from a research point of view and is it really desirable to preclude their occupants from normal participation in the full range of academic life?

The universities themselves should see to it that teaching assistantships are fully competitive with research assistantships and fellowships.

4. Federal agencies should provide space and equipment for their postdoctoral fellows and research career professors and for all contracts and most grants without the requirement of matching funds. It is very difficult to obtain space and equipment for these purposes from either endowments or state support, and also not entirely appropriate.

5. A National Foundation for Higher Education

might well be created on the model of the National Science Foundation. It could serve as a focal point for the interests of higher education and make grants outside the province of the National Science Foundation. Such a foundation would need to explore carefully the areas where support would be most productive, and also the appropriate forms of support, as did the National Science Foundation with such skill and judgment in its fields of interest. Areas for possible early consideration, as examples, are the creative arts, international studies, and environmental planning. Each is at a stage of considerable activity; each carries a high degree of national interest. Additionally, a Foundation for Higher Education might well undertake the support of great regional library resources with union catalogues made available to other university and college libraries in the region.

6. A number of other federal programs now in effect to aid higher education have generally worked well and should be continued.

The established program of the Federal Housing Authority in making loans for residence halls, student unions, and parking structures should be continued and expanded, as should the several programs under the National Defense Education Act. These programs are all widely dispersed in their efforts, and affect nearly all universities and many colleges.

Graduate fellowship programs should be expanded as there are capable graduate students to fill them. The availability of money does not by itself create a supply of competent candidates. At least half of the graduate fellowships should be transferable on a national basis, and not more than half tied to particular institutions. The practice of the Rockefeller Foundation and Woodrow Wilson Foundation of making an institutional grant to cover part of the institutional expenses for each scholar might well be more widely emulated.

The great need for curriculum reform in many fields, caused by the changing content and structure of knowledge growing out of research, should be recognized by federal agencies. They should support the efforts of universities to re-examine and improve the teaching in these areas. Some support is being given, particularly by the National Science Foundation in the physical sciences, but unfortunately some recent developments run counter to this trend. For example, the National Institutes of Health now cannot support any such efforts in the biological sciences—an area where they are greatly needed.

Foreign service projects conducted by universities for the federal government appear to be most fruitful if there is a major institutional assignment for a substantial period of time. *Ad hoc* projects accomplish little for the foreign country or for the contracting university.

7. Medical and dental doctors are in short supply

and will be in shorter supply. Fellowships and facilities for their training deserve high federal priority.[30]

8. A Council of Advisers on Education, as suggested by the American Assembly in 1960,[31] would provide an opportunity for an over-all view of the educational system and the educational needs of the nation as no single agency can do. This would be something like the President's Council of Economic Advisers, but in the educational field. Education may well need a better-coordinated voice than it has had, as McGeorge Bundy has so eloquently argued,[32] but the federal government also may need a more coordinated ear.

This council might assist in the preparation of a manpower budget covering the supply of, and demand for, the skills that depend on formal education. Indeed, beyond this the nation might benefit from an over-all manpower budget, supplementing its other budgets, for it would focus attention on human resources and on the importance of developing them.

The partnership of the federal government with higher education and particularly with the federal grant universities over the last two decades has been enormously productive in enlarging the pool of scientific ideas and skills. Now we are entering a new phase of widening and deepening relationships. This new phase can carry the American commitment to education to new heights of endeavor. It can also preserve the traditional freedom of higher education from excessive control. It can enlarge the horizons of equality of opportunity. It can maintain and even increase the margin for excellence. The challenge is to make certain it does all these things.

3

THE FUTURE OF THE CITY OF INTELLECT

"THE true American University," David Starr Jordan once observed, "lies in the future." It still does; for American universities have not yet developed their full identity, their unique theory of purpose and function. They still look to older and to foreign models, although less and less; and the day is coming when these models will no longer serve at all.

The task of prophecy is made difficult by the many internal and external cross-currents to which universities are exposed. Archibald MacLeish wrote in 1941: "Like other private institutions, Harvard must face the fact that gifts to the university in the foreseeable future will not equal in bulk the gifts of the late twenties. Like other private institutions, it must admit that the peak of enrollment has probably been reached. And like other private institutions it must therefore accept the fact that this period of its history will be a period of organization within existing frontiers, rather than a period of extension of existing frontiers."[1] Since 1941 Harvard has become a federal grant university, has obtained private gifts beyond previous experience, has expanded far beyond its then "existing frontiers." This illustration serves to demonstrate that prophecy has its perils when treating with as dynamic an institution in as changing an environment as the modern American university.

THE SECOND TRANSFORMATION

The American university is currently undergoing its second great transformation. The first occurred during roughly the last quarter of the nineteenth century, when the land grant movement and German intellectualism were together bringing extraordinary change. The current transformation will cover roughly the quarter century after World War II. The university is being called upon to educate previously unimagined numbers of students; to respond to the expanding claims of national service; to merge its activities with industry as never before; to adapt to and rechannel new intellectual currents. By the end of this period, there will be a truly American university, an institution unique in world history, an institution not looking to other models but serving, itself, as a model for universities in other parts of the globe. This is not said in boast.

It is simply that the imperatives that have molded the American university are at work around the world.

Each nation, as it has become influential, has tended to develop the leading intellectual institutions of its world—Greece, the Italian cities, France, Spain, England, Germany, and now the United States. The great universities have developed in the great periods of the great political entities of history. Today, more than ever, education is inextricably involved in the quality of a nation. It has been estimated that over the last thirty years nearly half of our national growth can be explained by the greater education of our people and by better technology, which is also largely a product of the educational system.[2]

So many of the hopes and fears of the American people are now related to our educational system and particularly to our universities—the hope for longer life, for getting into outer space, for a higher standard of living; our fears of Russian or Chinese supremacy, of the bomb and annihilation, of individual loss of purpose in the changing world. For all these reasons and others, the university has become a prime instrument of national purpose. This is new. This is the essence of the transformation now engulfing our universities.

The knowledge industry. Basic to this transformation is the growth of the "knowledge industry," which is coming to permeate government and business and to draw into it more and more people raised to higher and higher levels of skill. The production, distribution, and consumption of "knowledge" in all its forms is said to account for 29 percent of gross national product, according to Fritz Machlup's calculations; and "knowledge production" is growing at about twice the rate of the rest of the economy.[3] Knowledge has certainly never in history been so central to the conduct of an entire society. What the railroads did for the second half of the last century and the automobile for the first half of this century may be done for the second half of this century by the knowledge industry: that is, to serve as the focal point for national growth. And the university is at the center of the knowledge process.

The university historically has been growing in concentric circles. It started with philosophy in Greece, and a library—the first great one—at Alexandria. It spread to the ancient professions, and then to science. It permeated agriculture and now industry. Originally it served the elites of society, then the middle class as well, and now it includes the children of all, regardless of social and economic background.

Spatially the modern university often reflects its history, with the library and the humanities and social sciences at the center of the campus, extending out to the professional schools and scientific laboratories, and surrounded by industry, interspersed with residence halls, apartments, and boarding houses. An almost ideal location for a modern university is to be sandwiched between a middle-class district on its way to becoming a slum and an ultramodern industrial park—so that the students may live in the one and the faculty consult in the other. M.I.T. finds itself happily ensconced between the decaying sections of Cambridge and Technology Square.

Universities have become "bait" to be dangled in front of industry, with drawing power greater than low taxes or cheap labor. Route 128 around Boston and the great developing industrial complexes in the San Francisco Bay Area and Southern California reflect the universities in these areas. The Gilpatric report for the Department of Defense explained that 41 percent of defense contracts for research in the fiscal year 1961 were concentrated in California, 12 percent in New York, and 6 percent in Massachusetts, for a total of nearly 60 percent, in part because these were also "centers of learning." [4] Sterling Forest outside New York City seeks to attract industry by location next to a new university campus. [5] In California, new industrial laboratories were located next to two new university campuses before the first building was built on either of these campuses.

Sometimes industry will reach into a university laboratory to extract the newest ideas almost before they are born. Instead of waiting outside the gates, agents are working the corridors. They also work the placement offices. And the university, in turn, reaches into industry, as through the Stanford Research Institute.

The new connection of the university with the rise and fall of industrial areas has brought about an inter-university and interregional competition unmatched in history except by the universities and their *Länder* in nineteenth-century Germany. Texas and Pittsburgh seek to imitate what California and Boston have known; so also do Iowa, Seattle, and nearly all the rest. A vast campaign is on to see that the university center of each industrial complex shall not be "second best."

It is often through new academic specialties and through athletics that the universities seeking to rise in the academic hierarchy can most quickly and easily attract national attention—and also by hiring great and visible academic stars. The mark of a university "on the make" is a mad scramble for football stars and professorial luminaries. The former do little studying and the latter little teaching, and so they form a neat combination of muscle and intellect.

The university and segments of industry are becoming more alike. As the university becomes tied into the world of work, the professor—at least in the natural and some of the social sciences—takes on the characteristics of an entrepreneur. Industry, with its scientists and technicians, learns an uncomfortable bit about academic freedom and the handling of intellectual personnel. The two worlds are merging physically and psychologically.

The rise of Ideopolis. University centers have a tendency to coalesce. Allan Nevins has put it this way: "Observers of higher education can now foresee the inexorable emergence of an entirely new landscape. It will no longer show us a nation dotted by high academic peaks with lesser hills between; it will be a landscape dominated by mountain ranges." [6] The highest peaks of the future will rise from the highest plateaus.

One such plateau runs from Boston to Washington. At the universities and laboratories situated along this range are found 46 percent of the American Nobel Prize winners in the sciences and 40 percent of the members of the National Academy of Sciences. A second range with its peaks runs along the California coast. C. P. Snow has written: "And now the scientific achievement of the United States is moving at a rate we all ought to marvel at. Think of the astonishing constellation of talent, particularly in the physical sciences, all down the California coast, from Berkeley and Stanford to Pasadena and Los Angeles. There is nothing like that concentration of talent anywhere in the world. It sometimes surprises Europeans to realize how much of the pure science of the entire West is being carried out in the United States. Curiously enough, it often surprises Americans too. At a guess, the figure is something like 80 percent, and might easily be higher." [7]

The California mountain range has 36 percent of the Nobel laureates in science and 20 percent of the members of the National Academy of Sciences. The Big Ten and Chicago constitute a third range of academic peaks, with 10 percent of the Nobel laureates and 14 percent of the members of the National Academy of Sciences. These three groupings of universities—the East Coast, California, and the Big Ten and Chicago—currently produce over three quarters of the doctorates conferred in the United States. Another range may be in the process of development in the Texas-Louisiana area.

This concentration of talent partly follows history —the location of the older private and public universities. Partly it follows industrial strengths and population centers. But it also has its own logic. No one university can cover all specialties, or cover them well enough so that there is a sufficient cluster of close intellectual colleagues. The scholar dislikes intellectual isolation and good scholars tend to swarm together. These swarms are extraordinarily productive environments. No library can be complete; nor any graduate curriculum. Some laboratories, to be well used, must be used by more than one university. Thus the Big Ten and Chicago, through their Committee on Institutional Cooperation, are merging their library resources, creating a "common market" for graduate students, diversifying their research laboratories on a common-use basis, and parceling out foreign language specializations. Something similar is happening in the University of California system, and between Berkeley and Stanford. Harvard and M.I.T., Princeton and Pennsylvania, among others, run joint research enterprises.

These clustering universities, in turn, have clustering around them scientifically oriented industrial and governmental enterprises. To match the drawing power of the great metropolis, there now arrives the new Ideopolis. The isolated mountain can no longer dominate the landscape; the constellation is greater than the single star and adds to the brightness of the sky.

There are other possible patterns for development. France and Russia have not made their universities so central to the life of society. They have segregated their research institutes to a substantial degree and established separate institutions for much of their technical training. Also, both have set up their universities on a regional basis with one university having a monopoly in the region. Both France and Russia, however, are now making their universities more central mechanisms, and Paris and Moscow, in particular, are the dominating institutions. Nevertheless, their basic pattern is quite different from the American, and, I think, not as productive.

With these national, industrial, and academic

pulls upon them, universities need to be quickly responsive to opportunities, readily adaptable to change. Yet they are basically conservative institutions. Jacques Barzun in his *House of Intellect* presents this "House" from an inward looking and idealistic point of view, as one opposed to the "corruption" of science, to modern art, to foundations with their interdisciplinary projects, and so forth, regretting that the "House" is no longer "a company apart." [8] However, the "City of Intellect" of the modern university also must look outward and to reality; it cannot be "a company apart." This conflict between internal and external dynamics has always been a difficult one for universities but never so intense as at present when the imperatives of change press so unmercifully against the necessities of internal harmony.

CONSERVATIVE INSTITUTIONS—DYNAMIC ENVIRONMENT

There are two great clichés about the university. One pictures it as a radical institution, when in fact it is most conservative in its institutional conduct. The other pictures it as autonomous, a cloister, when the historical fact is that it has always responded, but seldom so quickly as today, to the desires and demands of external groups—sometimes for love, sometimes for gain, increasingly willingly, and, in some cases, too eagerly. The external view is that the university is radical; the internal reality is that it is conservative. The internal illusion is that it is a law unto itself; the external reality is that it is governed by history.

The university's gate of Janus leads inward as well as outward, and inside the gate the social landscape changes remarkably. When one looks inward toward the "ivory tower," he sees a different "looking-glass land." Here, to get somewhere, you must run twice as slowly. This is as it must be. The university, as an institution, needs to create an environment that gives to its faculty members:

a sense of stability—they should not fear constant change that distracts them from their work;

a sense of security—they should not need to worry about the attacks against them from outside the gate;

a sense of continuity—they should not be concerned that their work and the structure of their lives will be greatly disrupted;

a sense of equity—they should not be suspicious that others are being treated better than they are.

Inventiveness should be left to the individual faculty member within the protection and solidity of the surrounding institutional structure. Galileo within the conservative institution of Padua in his day, Erasmus at Oxford and Freiburg, Newton at Cambridge helped start the enormous metamorphosis from which the modern world emerged. But their institutions, as institutions, were stolidly changeless.

The faculty guild. "Nothing should ever be done for

the first time" was the wry conclusion of F. M. Cornford from his vantage point as a classicist at Cambridge University at the turn of the century when Cambridge was stirring with responses to the modern world. He added that "Nothing is ever done until every one is convinced that it ought to be done, and has been convinced for so long that it is now time to do something else."[9] John Stuart Mill had looked upon the British universities of his day as largely unrelated to the progress of national life. Harold Laski, a century after Mill, felt that Oxford and Cambridge operated under a form of "syndicalism," which he considered the antithesis of the social usefulness he sought, and that they were only partly saved by being shaken up by royal commissions every thirty or forty years. Flexner referred to universities generally as "institutions usually regarded as conservative, frequently even as strongholds of reaction," and added that "institutions as such tend for quite obvious reasons to lag behind the life which they express and further."[10]

With reference to the American scene, Frederick Rudolph in his recent authoritative study of American colleges and universities concluded that "Resistance to fundamental reform was ingrained in the American collegiate and university tradition, as over three hundred years of history demonstrated. . . . Except on rare occasions, the historic policy of the American college and university [was]: drift, reluctant accommodation, belated recognition that while no one was looking, change had in fact taken place." [11] Nevitt Sanford, after a study of more contemporary focus, observed that there have been few innovations at all and even fewer "initiated by college or university faculties"; when a movement for reform has come, "it is the collective faculty who usually seem to be dragging their feet." [12]

There is a kind of "guild mentality" in the academic profession, as in many others. The guild was isolationist toward society, devoted to producer as against consumer sovereignty, and committed more to guild rules than to quick adaptation to popular demand. The guild was egalitarian, full of senatorial courtesy, selective of its own members. It was also a "sort of club" as Snow has characterized the colleges of Cambridge and Oxford, [13] and an "oligarchy of senior professors" as Ashby has noted about these same institutions. [14] In Germany, the faculty was more a class structure than a guild—a class structure intimately tied into the class structure of the surrounding society, hierarchical rather than fraternal.

The self-contained guild idea is still an attractive ideal. One recent call to faculty members is to "close our gates," become "masters within our walls," assume a "posture of offence" against the surrounding society. [15] Yet, except in a few situations, the faculty guild has never been a fully self-governing guild in reality, and almost never a company of "free agents," [16] much as it might like to believe itself one. However, the guild idea, the "Republic of Scholars," is often and understandably the faculty member's vision of "pie-in-the-sky."

Some of history has swirled past the "guild"; some has disrupted it; some has transformed it; some has swept it entirely away. Much of the Renaissance occurred completely outside the university. The university was generally allied against the Reformation, although bitter fights were fought within many universities, and in some the reformers emerged triumphant. The industrial, democratic, and scientific revolutions have gradually moved in on the universities and changed them almost beyond recognition. Some revolutions, like the French and Russian, placed the "guild" fully under state control, although it has regained some of its ancient rights in France. In all of these intellectual and social revolutions, the university, as an institution, was initially more a "stronghold of reaction" than a revolutionary force, although the ideas of its individual members have often been a stimulus to change.

Eric Ashby has said that policy should "seep gradually upward" within the guild.[17] Sometimes it has. In Oxford and Cambridge, research of extraordinary quality developed when the guild was still in control and still devoted to the classics. But, generally, change, when it has come, has been initiated or at least assisted from outside the gates, as the case of England today so decisively demonstrates. The educational revolution now going on there comes from the outside and above, and finds its greatest proponents in the Labor Party.

The individual faculty member, and particularly the political liberal on the faculty, is often torn between the "guild" and the "socialist" views of the university. The guild view stands for self-determination, and for resistance against the administration and the trustees; the socialist view, for service to society which the administration and the trustees often represent. The guild view is elitist toward the external environment, conservative toward internal change, conformist in relation to the opinion of colleagues. The socialist view is democratic toward society, radical toward change, and nonconformist. And the political liberal is drawn toward both views. Here is a paradox. Few instituitions are so conservative as the universities about their own affairs while their members are so liberal about the affairs of others; and sometimes the most liberal faculty member in one context is the most conservative in another. The natural radical, within the context of the guild, is radically conservative. The faculty member who gets arrested as a "freedom rider" in the South is a flaming supporter of unanimous prior faculty consent to any change whatsoever on his campus in the North. The door to the faculty club leads both out and in.

Change is a traumatic experience for an academic community, as for others. The Yale faculty in 1828 rejected in theory, while proving in practice, that colleges "by being immovably moored to the same station . . . serve only to measure the rapid current of improvement which is passing by them." [18] In a very real sense, the faculty is the university—its most productive element, its source of distinction. And faculty members are properly partners in the enterprise with areas reserved for their exclusive control. Yet when change comes it is rarely at the instigation of this group of partners as a collective body. The group is more likely to accept or reject or comment, than to devise and propose. The group serves a purpose as a balance wheel—resisting some things that should be resisted, insisting on more thorough discussion of some things that should be more thoroughly discussed, delaying some developments where delay gives time to adjust more gracefully to the inevitable. All this yields a greater sense of order and stability.

Institutional changes are coming, however, in areas under faculty control or influence. Some of the needed revisions will be troublesome. In many places, curricula and calendars will need to be restudied; undergraduate teaching renovated; faculty concepts of equality of treatment revised; mechanization of some elements of instruction installed; some fields of study (like biology) revolutionized. These changes will come in the face of much faculty hesitation and even some resistance. At least two changes, however, will have faculty support. One will be directed toward overcoming the fractionalization of the intellectual world, and the other will call for procedures devised to make administration more personal, including faculty administration.

The faculty world seems to sense a loss of unity—intellectual and communal unity. In large measure this can be attributed to "the overwhelming predominance of things that are new over things that are old" and to what Robert Oppenheimer calls "a thinning of common knowledge." [19] Knowledge is now in so many bits and pieces and administration so distant that faculty members are increasingly figures in a "lonely crowd," intellectually and institutionally. It is a sad commentary on the "community of masters" when its elements come together in interchange only when they coalesce feverishly over a grievance about some episode related to a change of the calendar or a parking fee.

Quite fortunately, however, there is a kind of senatorial courtesy within the collective faculty about changes desired by a single member, or a few. Changes initiated from the outside, as in the development of the federal grant university, which also have their internal supporters, are especially easy to accomplish. The individual faculty member seeking something new has, in turn, often found his greatest encouragement and leverage coming from the outside; the individual scholar is the inventor, the outside agency the force for innovation. The inventing faculty member almost instinctively knows that internal change will come more easily if he obtains the external support of a foundation or a federal agency. These outside-to-inside and inside-to-outside alliances have been great sources of progress.

Much change also takes place largely outside collective faculty purview, outside the "veto groups" of the academic community—in the new department or institute, the new project, the new campus. The institute, in particular, has been as much the vehicle of innovation in recent years as the department has been the vault of tradition. Change comes more through spawning the new than reforming the old.

When change does come, it may be by the slow process of persuasion, or by subversion as through the inside-outside alliance, or by evasion as in the new enterprise, or by external decision. The academic community, regardless of the particular process involved, is more changed than changing; change is more unplanned than planned.

"Remembrance of things past." If the collective faculties represent the present, the collective alumni represent the past—as much the best of the past as the faculty the best of the present. The alumni are oriented toward their own undergraduate days. There seems to be a rising sense of alumni concern as the rate of change rises. Generally it is over the preservation of an emphasis on teaching as against research; of the beauty of the old campus as against the asphalt and concrete and glass of the recent

"improvements"; of the quality of remembered undergraduate life in its totality; of the old admission requirements which let the old grads get in; of athletic teams that never lost a game; of the spirit of the "halls of ivy" as against the technological materialism of the federal grant university; of the integrity of the old alma mater against the blandishments from Washington. The older and the smaller and the more private and the more distinguished the university, the greater the intensity of these concerns.

If the alumni are concerned, the undergraduate students are restless. Recent changes in the American university have done them little good—lower teaching loads for the faculty, larger classes, the use of substitute teachers for the regular faculty, the choice of faculty members based on research accomplishments rather than instructional capacity, the fragmentation of knowledge into endless subdivisions. There is an incipient revolt of undergraduate students against the faculty; the revolt that used to be against the faculty *in loco parentis* is now against the faculty *in absentia*. The students find themselves under a blanket of impersonal rules for admissions, for scholarships, for examinations, for degrees. It is interesting to watch how a faculty intent on few rules for itself can fashion such a plethora of them for the students. The students also want to be treated as distinct individuals.

If the faculty looks on itself as a guild, the undergraduate students are coming to look upon themselves more as a "class"; some may even feel like a "lumpen proletariat." Lack of faculty concern for teaching, endless rules and requirements, and impersonality are the inciting causes. A few of the "nonconformists" have another kind of revolt in mind. They seek, instead, to turn the university, on the. Latin American or Japanese models, into a fortress from which they can sally forth with impunity to make their attacks on society.

If federal grants for research brought a major revolution, then the resultant student sense of neglect may bring a minor counterrevolt, although the target of the revolt is a most elusive one.

The big state universities are most vulnerable to charges of neglect of students. The private universities, tied more to tradition, to student tuition, to alumni support, to smaller size, have generally far better preserved their devotion to undergraduate life.

In inter-university competition, the distribution of the ablest students, as shown by the statistics on scholarship winners, is a telling point. A university's share of the ablest students is an important element in its ranking: how attractive is its educational program to the students most entitled to make a choice?

Student pressures for better undergraduate instruction may be supplemented by the complaints of parents, who think their children are being sacrificed on the altar of research. Also, the public at large, whose attention has been riveted on the elementary and secondary schools as the "population bulge" has affected them, may now turn its attention increasingly to the university level when the "bulge" reaches there. Generally the public is more interested in quality of instruction than in quantity of research. The spotlight which the universities have helped turn on the teaching of others at lower levels may now be turned on their own.

External imperatives. The truly major changes in university life have been initiated from the outside, by such forces as Napoleon in France, ministers of education in Germany, royal commissions and the University Grants Committee in Great Britain, the Communist Party in Russia, the emperor at the time of the Restoration in Japan, the lay university governing boards and the federal Congress in the United States—and also, in the United States, by the foundations. The foundations, quickly responsive to needs and possibilities, have been the main instruments, for example, in the reform of medical education, the introduction of interdisciplinary studies, the involvement of universities in world affairs. As catalysts, their influence has been enormous. The new developments might have been undertaken within the universities themselves, but they were not.

Prospective changes can be identified, in part, by the interests of the external initiators—trustees, state governments, foundations, industry, the federal government. What are the current concerns? There are:

problems related to costs, identified particularly by Beardsley Ruml—faculty-student ratios, fuller utilization of the calendar, excessive numbers of courses, mechanization of instruction; [20]

problems related to accommodation of the vast numbers of young people already knocking on the doors;

problems related to public service—cultural programs, urban extension, advice to state and federal legislators and agencies;

problems related to the supply of trained personnel for industry and the public, particularly engineers, scientists, and doctors;

questions about the quality and availability of research, particularly the establishment of additional university research centers;

problems related to the exploitation of new discoveries, particularly in the biological sciences and spreading out into the health sciences and agriculture.

Additionally there is a general public concern with "morality" on the campus; with the so-called beatniks, with the young radicals, with cheating, and with sex. There is also a deep concern about how far, and how fast, research discoveries may change the lives of everyone. These "moral" concerns fill the incoming mailbox of the administrator.

The external origin of most changes raises very

grave problems: how to identify the "good" and the "bad," and how to embrace the good and resist the bad. There is also a problem of timing—how to adjust not too rapidly and not too slowly. And there are the problems of how to change the content of the university without changing its essential forms; of how to reconcile the conservatism of the collective faculty with the radical function of the total institution as carried out primarily by the individual faculty members. These obligations to select the good and reject the bad, to pace the rate of change, and to discover the methods of change that will do least damage to traditional processes fall primarily on the reluctant shoulders of the administrator. And as Cornford remarked: "You think (do you not?) that you have only to state a reasonable case, and people must listen to reason and act upon it at once. It is just this conviction that makes you so unpleasant." [21]

Today, changes are occurring quite rapidly and spontaneously. In addition, inter-university rivalry has become so intense that the rate of acceptance of change has been accelerated. The current problem is not so much that the university does not fully control the direction of its own development—it seldom has—but rather that it must make what are judged to be essential adjustments so often and so quickly, like an amoeba in an unfriendly environment. This has added to the strains placed on the internal structure of the institution. At the same time, however, the current rate of growth in numbers helps to relieve these strains, for a period of growth necessarily involves considerable flexibility. Still, the major test of the modern American university is how wisely and how quickly it adjusts to the important new possibilities. The great universities of the future will be those which have adjusted rapidly and effectively.

THE NEW FACES OF CHANGE

The universities are currently facing three great areas of related adjustments: growth, shifting academic emphases, and involvement in the life of society. The direction of adjustment in each of these areas is reasonably clear; the detailed arrangements and the timing are not.

1. *Growth*. The number of university and college students in the United States will almost double during the 1960's. This addition of three million will duplicate in one decade the growth of the three centuries since Harvard was founded. The proportion of graduate students will rise considerably, and there are already 25,000 postdoctoral students.

Existing campuses are being enlarged and many new ones founded. This will be the greatest period of campus renovation and establishment in American history. A particularly large number of junior colleges will be formed as the junior college movement becomes nationwide.

New centers of graduate strength are emerging, and a network of alliances is being formed among the old and the new centers in the competition to offer the greatest total combination of resources.

To accommodate the great increase in enrollments, many calendars are being rearranged, particularly in state-supported institutions, to permit more nearly year-round use of physical facilities. Students will be able to accelerate their work if they wish, and generally students will come and go with less reference to their "class"; more of them will drop in and drop out as suits their particular schedules and needs.

There will be some further mechanization of instruction (television, language laboratories, programmed learning) to improve quality and to save faculty time for other endeavors, including more individual work with students. The sciences will almost eagerly embrace these aids to learning. The foreign language departments will be rather reluctant, because these devices can threaten their structure of faculty employment and the recruitment and utilization of graduate students.

Because of the competition for faculty members, salaries will continue to rise; fringe benefits of all sorts will be devised to tie professors to a particular campus. In addition to competition among universities, there is also intensified competition with industry and government. This competition has obvious advantages in raising faculty income but it has its negative aspects. As the market becomes more active, internal equity will be injured, for some disciplines are much more in demand in the market than others. Teaching loads will be competitively reduced, sometimes to zero, although more teachers are needed and students are complaining about lack of attention. The identification of the professor with his university will be generally loosened—he will become more a member of a free-floating profession. The rules regarding how much time a professor can spend away from his university assignments and those affecting the sources of his income within the university will continue to be in great flux.

This current phenomenon of rising salaries and benefits, however, may be of relatively short duration, lasting, perhaps, for the remainder of this decade. Faculty salaries have been catching up with incomes in other professions after an historical lag. By 1970, also, the personnel deficit of today may be turning into the surplus of tomorrow as all the new Ph.D.'s roll into the market. A new plateau of compensation may be reached in the 1970's. But in the long run, it is common labor more than uncommon talent that is rising in its comparative monetary evaluation, as the educational process uncovers more talent and depletes the ranks of those willing to do common labor.

2. *Shifting academic emphases.* Knowledge is exploding along with population. There is also an ex-

plosion in the need for certain skills. The university is responding to all these explosions.

The vastly increased needs for engineers, scientists, and doctors will draw great resources to these areas of the university. Also, some new professions are being born. Others are becoming more formally professional, for example, business administration and social work. The university becomes the chief port of entry for these professions. In fact, a profession gains its identity by *making* the university the port of entry. This creates new roles for education; but it is also part of the process of freezing the structure of the occupational pyramid and assuring that the well-behaved do advance, even if the geniuses do not. The university is used as an egg-candling device; and it is, perhaps, a better one than any other that can be devised, but the process takes some of the adventure out of occupational survival, and does for some professions what the closed shop has done for some unions. The life of the universities for a thousand years has been tied into the recognized professions in the surrounding society, and the universities will continue to respond as new professions arise.

The fastest-growing intellectual field today is biology. Here there is a veritable revolution where the doctrine of evolution once reigned supreme. To the classifying efforts of the past are being added the new analytical methods of the present, often drawn from chemistry and physics. There are levels of complexity to be explored in all living structures. The "code of life" can now be read; soon it will be understood, and soon after that, used. It is an intellectual discovery of unique and staggering propportions. The secrets of the atom, much as they have changed and are changing human activity on this planet, may hold no greater significance than the secrets still hidden in the genetic code. If the first half of the twentieth century may be said to have belonged to the physical sciences, the second half may well belong to the biological. Resources within the universities will be poured into the new biology and into the resulting new medicine and agriculture, well supported though medicine and agriculture already are.

Another field ready to bloom is that of the creative arts, hitherto the ugly ducklings or Cinderellas of the academic world. America is bursting with creativity in painting, music, literature, the theater with a vigor equaled in few other parts of the world today. Italy, France, Spain, Germany, Russia, England, the Low Countries have had great periods of cultural flowering. America is having one now. In the arts the universities have been more hospitable to the historian and the critic than to the creator; he has found his havens elsewhere. Yet it is the creativity of science that has given science its prestige in the university. Perhaps creativity will do the same again for the humanities, though there may be less new to create than has recently been true in science and the tests of value are far less precise. A very important role remains for the historian of past ages of creativity and for the critic of the current productions. But the universities need to find ways also to accommodate pure creative effort if they are to have places on stage as well as in the wings and in the audience in the great drama of cultural growth now playing on the American stage.

These possibilities for expansion—in the training of engineers, scientists, doctors, and the newer professionals, in biology, and in the creative arts, among various others—raise again the problem of balance. As James Bryant Conant has noted, the Western world has had for a thousand years a continuing problem of "keeping a balance between the advancement of knowledge, professional education, general education, and the demands of student life." [22]

But the balance is always changing; this is the unbalancing reality. The balance is not equal treatment, the provision of equal time in some mechanical and eternal way between teaching and research, or between the humanities and science. The dynamics of balance did not give equal treatment to the available scientist in Padua in 1300 when Giotto was painting his chapel, or to the available artist in Padua in 1600 when Galileo was lecturing from his crude platform. Balance cannot be determined on the scales by blind justice, field versus field and activity versus activity.

The essence of balance is to match support with the intellectual creativity of subject fields; with the need for skills of the highest level; with the kinds of expert service that society currently most requires. None of these measures is constant. Balance requires, therefore, a shifting set of judgments which relates facilities and attention to the possibilities inherent in each field, each skill, each activity at that moment of time in that environment, yet preserves for all fields their essential integrity. To know balance is to know the potential creativity, the potential productivity, the potential contribution of each competing activity in an unfolding pattern of time and an evolving landscape of environment. To know balance is to know more than anyone can ever know in advance. But decisions must nevertheless be made and time will tell how well. The only certainly wrong decision is that the balance of today must be preserved for tomorrow. Where will the world's work and the university's work best be done? The answer to that question is the true definition of balance.

3. *Involvement in the life of society*. Knowledge is now central to society. It is wanted, even demanded, by more people and more institutions than ever before. The university as producer, wholesaler and retailer of knowledge cannot escape service. Knowledge, today, is for everybody's sake.

The campus and society are undergoing a somewhat reluctant and cautious merger, already well advanced. M.I.T. is at least as much related to industry and government as Iowa State ever was to agriculture. Extension work is really becoming "life-long learning." Harvard today has four postgraduate doctors in its medical school for every one still working for his degree; so also for many other skills including business. Television makes it possible for extension to reach into literally every home; the boundaries of the university are stretched to embrace all of society. The student becomes alumnus and the alumnus continues as student; the graduate enters the outside world and the public enters the classroom and the laboratory. Knowledge has the terrifying potential of becoming popular, opening a Pandora's box.

The campus becomes a center for cultural life; it has a ready-made audience in its students and faculty and it has the physical facilities. Persons attracted by the performing and visual arts and the lectures come to live around the campus—also assorted crackpots. As the downtown area in some cities decays, the campus takes its place as the cultural center of the community. A new dimension has been added to the land grant idea of service.

The New Deal took professors to Washington from many campuses, the New Frontier from more than just one. In Wisconsin before World War I, the campus and the state house in Madison were exceptionally close. Today the campus is being drawn to the city hall and the state capitol as never before. The politicians need new ideas to meet the new problems; the agencies need expert advice on how to handle the old. The professor can supply both. Keynes concluded his *General Theory* as follows: ". . . the ideas of economists and political philosophers, both when they are right and when they are wrong, are more powerful than is commonly understood. Indeed the world is ruled by little else. Practical men, who believe themselves to be quite exempt from any intellectual influences, are usually the slaves of some defunct economist. Madmen in authority, who hear voices in the air, are distilling their frenzy from some academic scribbler of a few years back. I am sure that the power of vested interests is vastly exaggerated compared with the gradual encroachment of ideas." [23] As, for example, the ideas of Keynes.

The university must range itself on the side of intelligent solutions to sometimes unintelligent questions. These questions more and more arise from abroad as well as at home; and the quality of the answers has been made all the more crucial in a world swept by Communist and nationalist revolutions.

There are those who fear the further involvement of the university in the life of society. They fear that the university will lose its objectivity and its freedom. But society is more desirous of objectivity and more tolerant of freedom than it used to be. The university can be further ahead of the times and further behind the times, further to the left of the public and further to the right of the public—and still keep its equilibrium—than was ever the case before, although problems in this regard are not yet entirely unknown. There are those who fear that the university will be drawn too far from basic to applied research and from applied research to application itself. But the lines dividing these never have been entirely clear and much new knowledge has been generated at the borders of basic and applied research, and even of applied knowledge and its application.

Growth and shifting emphases and involvement in society all take money; and which universities get it in the largest quantities will help determine which of them excel a decade or two hence. Will federal support be spent according to merit or according to political power? Will private donors continue to do as well as they recently have for those universities that have done well already? Will the states find new sources of revenue or will their expenditures be held under a lid of no new taxes? The answers to these questions will help predict the standings on the next rating scale of universities.

However this turns out, the scene of American higher education will continue to be marked by great variety, and this is one of its great strengths. The large and the small, the private and the public, the general and the specialized all add their share to over-all excellence. The total system is extraordinarily flexible, decentralized, competitive—and productive. The new can be tried, the old tested with considerable skill and alacrity. Pluralism in higher education matches the pluralistic American society. The multiversity, in particular, is the child of middle-class pluralism; it relates to so much of the variety of the surrounding society and is thus so varied internally.

The general test of higher education is not how much is done poorly, and some is; rather it is how much is done superbly, and a great deal is, to the nation's great benefit. Although it has been said that the best universities in America have been caught in a "stalemate of success," [24] there is no stalemate; there is some success.

CHANGES STILL TO COME

There has been some success, but there are some problems still to be fully faced; and they are problems of consequence.

One is the improvement of undergraduate instruction in the university. It will require the solution of many sub-problems: how to give adequate recognition to the teaching skill as well as to the research performance of the faculty; how to create a curriculum that serves the needs of the student as well as the research interests of the teacher; how to prepare the generalist as well as the specialist in an age of specialization looking for better generalizations; how to treat the individual student as a unique human being in the mass student body; how to make the university seem smaller even as it grows larger; how to establish a range of contact between faculty and students broader than the one-way route across the lectern or through the television screen; how to raise educational policy again to the forefront of faculty concerns. Increasingly, also, the better institutions will need to keep in mind that many of their undergraduate students will be going on to graduate school, and therefore that they need individual attention as pre-graduate students.

Another major task is to create a more unified intellectual world. We need to make contact between the two, the three, the many cultures; to open channels of intelligent conversation across the disciplines and divisions; to close the gap between C. P. Snow's "Luddites" and scientists;[25] to answer fragmentation with general theories and sensitivities. Even philosophy, which once was the hub of the intellectual universe, is now itself fragmented into such diverse specialties as mathematics and semantics. However, the physical sciences are drawing together as new discoveries create more basic general theories; the biological sciences may be pulled together in the process now going on; the social sciences might be unified around the study of organizations and the relations of individuals to and within them. Chemistry and social psychology may come to be central focalizing fields. As knowledge is drawn together, if in fact it is, a faculty may again become a community of masters; but "a sense of the unity . . . of all knowledge" [26] is still a very long way off.

A third problem is to relate administration more directly to individual faculty and students in the massive institution. We need to decentralize below the campus level to the operating agencies; to make the collective faculty a more vital, dynamic, progressive force as it now is only at the departmental level; to bridge the growing chasm between the department that does the teaching and the institute that does the research, with the faculty member torn between; to make the old departments and divisions more compatible with the new divisions of knowledge; to make it possible for an institution to see itself in totality rather than just piecemeal and in the sweep of history rather than just at a moment of time; to bring an understanding of both internal and external realities to all those intimately related to the process, so that there may be greater understanding; to see to it that administration serves and stimulates rather than rules the institution, that it be expendable when necessary and flexible all the time; to assure that the university can do better what it does best: to solve the whole range of governmental problems within the university.

Additionally, there is the urgent issue of how to preserve a margin for excellence in a populist society, when more and more of the money is being spent on behalf of all of the people. The great university is of necessity elitist—the elite of merit—but it operates in an environment dedicated to an egalitarian philosophy. How may the contribution of the elite be made clear to the egalitarians, and how may an aristocracy of intellect justify itself to a democracy of all men? It was equality of opportunity, not equality *per se,* that animated the founding fathers and the progress of the American system; but the forces of populist equality have never been silent, the battle between Jeffersonianism and Jacksonianism never finally settled.

If there are to be new departures, they are most likely to come on the campuses of those old, private universities which have prided themselves on control of their own destiny, and on the totally new campuses of the state universities in America and the new public universities in Britain. The university for the twenty-first century is more likely to emerge from these environments than from any others. Out of the pride of the old and the vacuum of the new may come the means to make undergraduate life more exciting, intellectual discourse more meaningful, administration more human. And perhaps there will arise a more dynamic demonstration of how excellence makes democracy more vital and its survival more assured. Then the universities may rise to "the heights of the times" and overcome "their inspirational poverty." [27]

George Beadle, president of the University of Chicago, once implied that the very large American university (but not his own) might be like the dinosaur which "became extinct because he grew larger and larger and then sacrificed the evolutionary flexibility he needed to meet changing conditions";[28] its body became too large for its brain. David Riesman has spoken of the leading American universities as "directionless . . . as far as major innovations are concerned";[29] they have run out of foreign models to imitate; they have lost their "ferment." The fact is that they are not directionless; they have been moving in clear directions and with considerable speed; there has been no "stalemate." But these directions have not been set as much by the university's visions of its destiny as by the external environment, including the federal government, the foundations, the surrounding and sometimes engulfing industry.

The university has been embraced and led down the garden path by its environmental suitors; it has been so attractive and so accommodating; who could resist it and why would it, in turn, want to resist?

But the really new problems of today and tomorrow may lend themselves less to solutions by external authority; they may be inherently problems for internal resolution. The university may now again need to find out whether it has a brain as well as a body.

We have been speaking of the City of Intellect as a university city with its satellite suburbs. The City of Intellect may be viewed in a broader context, encompassing all the intellectual resources of a society, and the even broader perspective of the force of intellect as the central force of a society— its soul. Will it be the salvation of our society?

The organized intellect is a great machine that has gained extraordinary momentum since the Greeks got it going 2500 years ago. It turns out its countless new pieces of knowledge but with little thought for their consequences—their impact on the environment—like a new insecticide. Its attention to problems quite naturally does not always relate primarily to their importance but often, instead, to the possibility of their solution. Thus the problems of rising population and rising levels of destructive capacity move along without study commensurate with their inherent significance. Does this machine have within it the "seeds of its own destruction"? Or can it develop an over-all rationality? As Lee DuBridge of Cal Tech has said: "Scientists and engineers do worry about the consequences of their

works. But neither they nor anyone else has discovered how to avoid or even to predict these consequences." [30]

The process cannot be stopped. The results cannot be foreseen. It remains to adapt. And here the
social sciences and humanities may find their particular roles in helping to define the good as well as
the true and to add wisdom to truth. It may not be
the conflict of cultures that is so crucial but rather
the rate at which each culture moves forward. Can
the intellect come to handle all the problems it
creates in the course of solving other problems? Can
the university help solve the growing war between
the future and the past? Can the span of intellectual
comprehension be widened spatially and tempo-
rally?

Intellect has also become an instrument of national purpose, a component part of the "military-
industrial complex." Our Western City of Intellect
finds its counterpart or counterparts in the East.
In the war of the ideological worlds, a great deal
depends on the use of this instrument. Knowledge
is durable. It it also transferable. Knowledge costs
a great deal to produce, less to reproduce. Thus it
only pays to produce knowledge if through production it can be put into use better and faster. The
Communist City of Intellect has been a planned
community. It grows only in certain directions and
in certain ways. This allows concentration of effort
but limits growth and recognition except in re-

stricted segments of the intellectual world. This
City flourishes in science and in military might but
lags in the humanities and the social sciences. Whole
areas that would be covered by a really modern
City of Intellect are largely unpopulated.

The two Cities of Intellect are not only sources
of weapons— they also form a potential bridge between their two societies. Knowledge is universal.
Its creators generally prefer freedom. To the extent
the Eastern City of Intellect grows and makes contact with the Western, it almost inevitably changes
its own society. Here a certain type of society really
may carry the "seeds of its own destruction." It
either competes and changes, or it loses some of its
over-all power of competition.

Marx saw technology as the major force in history; but intellect creates technology and the logic
of intellect's development may be quite different
from the unraveling of the "mode of production" as
Marx visualized it. History has seldom, if ever,
proved a theorist to be so incorrect and at the same
time so influential as Marx. The wave of the future
may more nearly be middle-class democracy,[31]
with all its freedoms, through its better use of intellect in all intellect's many dimensions, than the
"dictatorship of the proletariat" (which, in fact, is
the dictatorship of the single party). But it has not
yet been proved conclusively whether intellect can
preserve and even create the culture of freedom, in
which it best flourishes, more effectively than tech-

nology, under Communist leadership, can be used to bolster dictatorship.

The intellect, and the university as its most happy home, can have great potential roles to play in the reconciliation of the war between the future and the past, and the solution—one way or the other— of the war between the ideological giants who now rend the world with their struggles. Certain it is, however, that the reconciliation of the future and the past can only be made more elusive in the context of an ideological struggle where survival is almost the sole essence of rational behavior. The two problems compound each other's effects.

At the outset I quoted Cardinal Newman on his "Idea of a University," reflecting the beautiful ivory tower of Oxford as it once was. It seems appropriate to conclude with Alfred North Whitehead's prophetic words in 1916 on the place of intellect: "In the conditions of modern life, the rule is absolute: the race which does not value trained intelligence is doomed. Not all your heroism, not all your social charm, not all your wit, not all your victories on land or sea, can move back the finger of fate. Today we maintain ourselves. Tomorrow science will have moved forward yet one more step, and there will be no appeal from the judgment which will be pronounced on the uneducated."[32]

These are the uses of the university.

NOTES

Chapter 1: The Idea of a Multiversity

[1] John Henry Cardinal Newman, *The Idea of a University* (New York: Longmans Green and Co., 1947). The quotations used here are from pp. 129, 91, xxvii, 157.

[2] Francis Bacon, "The Advancement of Learning," *Essays, Advance of Learning, New Atlantic and Other Places* (New York: Odyssey Press, Inc., 1937), pp. 214–215.

[3] Abraham Flexner, *Universities: American English German* (New York: Oxford University Press, 1930). The quotations are from pp. 3, 4, 42, 179, 132, 25, 44–45, 197, 193, 231, 235, 197 (again), 178–179.

[4] Harvard University, *The President's Report, 1961–62,* p. 3.

[5] Hastings Rashdall, *The Universities of Europe in the Middle Ages* (3 vols., 1895, ed. F. M. Powicke and A. B. Emden, Oxford: Clarendon Press, 1936), III, 358.

[6] Benjamin Franklin, *Proposals Relating to the Education of Youth in Pensilvania* (Philadelphia, 1749).

[7] *Reports of the Course of Instruction in Yale College by a Committee of the Corporation and the Academical Faculty* (New Haven, Conn.: Hezekiah Howe, 1828).

[8] Allan Nevins, *The State Universities and Democracy* (Urbana: University of Ilinois Press, 1962), p. vi.

[9] John J. Corson, *Governance of Colleges and Universities* (New York: McGraw-Hill, 1960), pp. 175–179.

[10] José Ortega y Gassett, *The Mission of the University* (London: Kegan Paul, Trench, Trubner and Co., Ltd., 1946), p. 56.

[11] McGeorge Bundy, "Of Winds and Windmills: Free Universities and Public Policy," in Charles G. Dobbins, ed., *Higher Education and the Federal Government, Programs and Problems* (Washington, D.C.: American Council on Education, 1963), p. 93.

[12] *General Education in a Free Society,* Report of the Harvard Committee with an Introduction by James Bryant Conant (Cambridge, Mass.: Harvard University Press, 1945).

[13] Richard Hofstadter and Walter P. Metzger, *The Development of Academic Freedom in the United States* (New York: Columbia University Press, 1955), pp. 71, 61.

[14] Thorstein Veblen, *The Higher Learning in America* (Stanford, Calif.: Academic Reprints, 1954), p. 85.

[15] Upton Sinclair, *The Goose-Step: A Study of American Education* (Pasadena: John Regan & Co., 1923), pp. 382–384.

[16] Robert Maynard Hutchins, *Freedom, Education and The Fund: Essays and Addresses, 1946–1956* (New York: Meridian Books, 1956), pp. 167–196.

[17] Harold W. Dodds, *The Academic President—Educator or Caretaker?* (New York: McGraw-Hill, 1962).

[18] Frederick Rudolph, *The American College and University: A History* (New York: Alfred A. Knopf, 1962), p. 492.

[19] James Lewis Morrill, *The Ongoing State University* (Minneapolis: University of Minnesota Press, 1960), p. 48.

[20] John D. Millett, *The Academic Community: An Essay on Organization* (New York: McGraw-Hill, 1962), p. 259.

[21] Henry M. Wriston, *Academic Procession: Reflections of a College President* (New York: Columbia University Press, 1959), p. 172.

[22] Eric Ashby, "The Administrator: Bottleneck or Pump?" *Daedalus,* Spring 1962, pp. 264–278.

[23] Hutchins, pp. 177, 169.

[24] A. Lawrence Lowell, *What a University President Has Learned* (New York: Macmillan, 1938), pp. 12, 19.

[25] Rudolph, p. 291.

[26] James Morris, "Is Oxford Out of This World?" *Horizon,* January 1963, p. 86.

[27] James Bryce, *The American Commonwealth,* new edition (New York: Macmillan, 1914), II, 718–719.

[28] Paul F. Lazarsfeld, "The Sociology of Empirical Social Research," *American Sociological Review,* December 1962, pp. 751–767.

[29] David Riesman, *Constraint and Variety in American Education* (Garden City, N.Y.: Doubleday, 1958), pp. 30–32.

[30] Ernest Earnest, *Academic Procession* (Indianapolis: Bobbs-Merrill, 1953), p. 74.

[31] Rudolph, p. 423.

[32] Eric Ashby, "Self-Government in Modern British Universities," *Science and Freedom,* December 1956, p. 10.

[33] Theodore Caplow and Reece J. McGee, *The Academic Marketplace* (New York: Basic Books, 1958), p. 206.

[34] Millett, p. 224.

[35] Wriston, p. 172.

[36] Nevins, pp. 118–119.

[37] Dodds, p. 43.

[38] W. Max Wise, *They Come For the Best of Reasons—College Students Today* (Washington, D.C.: American Council on Education, 1958).

[39] Burton R. Clark and Martin Trow, *Determinants of College Student Subculture,* unpublished manuscript, Center for the Study of Higher Education, University of California, Berkeley, 1963.

[40] Robert Bendiner, "The Non-Teacher," *Horizon,* September 1962, p. 14.

[41] Merle A. Tuve, "Is Science Too Big for the Scientist?" *Saturday Review,* June 6, 1959, p. 49.

CHAPTER 2: The Realities of the Federal Grant University

[1] Don K. Price, "The Scientific Establishment," *Science,* June 29, 1962.

[2] Some of the principal reports, 1960–1963, are as follows:
American Assembly, *The Federal Government and Higher Education* (Englewood Cliffs, N.J.: Prentice-Hall, 1960).
Homer D. Babbidge, Jr., and Robert M. Rosenzweig, *The*

Federal Interest in Higher Education (New York: McGraw-Hill, 1962).

William G. Bowen, *The Federal Government and Princeton University: A Report on the Effects of Princeton's Involvements with the Federal Government on the Operations of the University* (Princeton University, 1962).

Julius H. Comroe. Jr., ed., *Research and Medical Education* (Evanston, Ill.: Association of American Medical Colleges, 1962).

Charles G. Dobbins, ed., *Higher Education and the Federal Government, Programs and Problems* (Washington, D.C.: American Council on Education, 1963).

Harvard and the Federal Government: A Report to the Faculties and Governing Boards of Harvard University (Harvard University, September 1961).

Charles V. Kidd, *American Universities and Federal Research* (Cambridge, Mass.: The Belknap Press of Harvard University Press, 1959).

J. Kenneth Little, *A Survey of Federal Programs in Higher Education: Summary Describing the Programs, Participating Institutions, and the Effects of the Programs on the Institutions* (Washington, D.C.: Government Printing Office, 1962).

Harold Orlans, *The Effects of Federal Programs on Higher Education: A Study of 36 Universities and Colleges* (Washington, D.C.: Brookings Institution, 1962).

Alice M. Rivlin, *The Role of the Federal Government in Financing Higher Education* (Washington, D.C.: Brookings Institution, 1961).

Glenn T. Seaborg *et al.*, *Scientific Progress, the Universities and the Federal Government: A Statement by the President's Science Advisory Committee*, Nov. 15, 1960.

[3] These fourteen specialized research centers are:

Columbia Radiation Laboratory (Columbia)—Department of Defense.

Applied Physics Laboratory (Johns Hopkins)—Department of the Navy.

Hudson Laboratories (Columbia)—Department of the Navy.

Lincoln Laboratory (M.I.T.)—Department of the Air Force.

Argonne National Laboratory (Chicago)—Atomic Energy Commission.

Cambridge Electron Accelerator (Harvard and M.I.T.)—Atomic Energy Commission.

Lawrence Radiation Laboratory (California)—Atomic Energy Commission.

Los Alamos Scientific Laboratory (California)—Atomic Energy Commission.

Princeton-Pennsylvania Proton Accelerator (Princeton and Pennsylvania)—Atomic Energy Commission.

Princeton Stellerator (Princeton)—Atomic Energy Commission.

Jet Propulsion Laboratory (California Institute of Technology)—National Aeronautics and Space Administration.

Brookhaven National Laboratory (Associated Universities, Inc.)—National Science Foundation.

Kitt Peak Observatory (Association of Universities for Research in Astronomy)—National Science Foundation.

Green Bank Radio Astronomy Observatory (Associated Universities, Inc.)—National Science Foundation and Department of the Air Force.

[4] Sidney Hook, "The Impact of Expanding Research Support on the Universities," in Comroe, ed., pp. 235–237.

[5] Malcolm Moos and Francis E. Rourke, *The Campus and the State* (Baltimore: Johns Hopkins Press, 1959).

[6] See James B. Handler, "An Optimistic View," in Comroe, ed., p. 108: "When asked, they much prefer judgment by a jury in Washington to the risk of judgment by colleagues at home."

[7] Homer D. Babbidge, Jr., and Robert M. Rosenzweig, "The Issues," *The Graduate Journal,* University of Texas, vol. V (1962), Supplement, pp. 62–104.

[8] Dael Wolfle, *America's Resources of Specialized Talent* (New York: Harper, 1954), pp. 190–191, 317–322.

[9] Orlans, p. 173.

[10] Hook, p. 238.

[11] Orlans, p. 134.

[12] J. A. Stratton, "Research and the University," *Chemical and Engineering News,* vol. 31, no. 25 (June 22, 1953), pp. 2582–2583.

[13] Nathan Pusey, "The Carnegie Study," in Dobbins, ed., p. 25.

[14] Don K. Price, *Government and Science* (New York: New York University Press, 1954), p. 96.

[15] Logan Wilson, "A New Dimension," *The Graduate Journal,* University of Texas, vol. V (1962), Supplement, p. 164.

[16] Seaborg *et al.,* as cited in note 2, above. See also in this connection the Report of the President's Science Advisory Committee, *Meeting Manpower Needs in Science and Technology: Graduate Training in Engineering, Mathematics, and Physical Sciences,* Dec. 12, 1962.

[17] Roswell L. Gilpatric, *The Changing Patterns of Defense Procurement,* issued by the Office of the Secretary of Defense, June 19, 1962.

[18] *Circular Letter No. 4,* Association of State Universities and Land-Grant Colleges (Washington, D.C., Feb. 13, 1963).

[19] "The situation appears to call for general aid to U.S. universities patterned somewhat after that provided universities in the United Kingdom by the University Grants Committee. In any event, the question arises of direct subsidy to educational institutions in order to increase the over-all strength of their departments and to provide greater flexibility in their administration." National Science Foundation, *Annual Report, 1960,* p. 16.

Also, Sidney Hook, in Comroe, ed., p. 245, says, "Personally, I see the best solution—not the ideal solution, for there is none—in the system that today obtains in England, where through the University Grants Committee the government makes lump grants to universities that are not earmarked for specific purposes. This system would give a university the necessary autonomy to meet educational needs as it sees them, and permit the deployment of resources at the key points of its educational enterprise."

[20] John Walsh, "Congress: Lag in Science Advice Gives Executive an Advantage," *Science,* vol. 139, no. 3549 (Jan. 4, 1963), p. 27.

[21] *Harvard and the Federal Government,* p. 26.

[22] Basil O'Connor, "Science and Government—The Perilous

Partnership," speech delivered Jan. 16, 1963, at the Third Symposium on Immunopathology, La Jolla, Calif.

[23] President John F. Kennedy, *Message on Education,* Jan. 29, 1963.

[24] Orlans, p. 169. It might be noted that the designations "public" and "private" have considerably less meaning for the federal grant universities than they once did for institutions of higher education.

[25] Orlans, p. 264.

[26] Charles V. Kidd, "The Institute Discussion: Research Emphasis and Research Itself," in Comroe, ed., p. 120.

[27] Orlans, p. 180.

[28] Alvin M. Weinberg, "Criteria for Scientific Choice," *Minerva,* Winter 1962.

[29] See *Report to the President on Government Contracting for Research and Development,* prepared by the Bureau of the Budget and referred to the Committee on Government Operations, United States Senate, May 17, 1962; and *Operation and Management of Research and Development Facilities and Programs, Analytical and Advisory Services and Technical Supervision of Weapons Systems and Other Programs for the Government, In-House and by Contract,* prepared by a committee under the chairmanship of Helge Holst, treasurer and corporate counsel of Arthur D. Little, Inc., and dated April 17, 1962.

[30] See the White House special message, *Improving American Health,* Feb. 7, 1963.

[31] American Assembly (note 2, above), p. 199.

[32] McGeorge Bundy, "Of Winds and Windmills: Free Universities and Public Policy," in Dobbins, ed. (note 2, above), pp. 96–98.

CHAPTER 3: The Future of the City of Intellect

[1] Archibald MacLeish, *The Next Harvard* (Cambridge, Mass.: Harvard University Press, 1941), p. 4.

[2] Edward F. Denison, *Sources of Economic Growth in the United*

States (New York: Committee for Economic Development, 1962).

³ Fritz Machlup, *The Production and Distribution of Knowledge in the United States* (Princeton, N.J.: Princeton University Press, 1962), pp. 374, 399.

⁴ Roswell L. Gilpatric, *The Changing Patterns of Defense Procurement,* issued by the Office of the Secretary of Defense, June 19, 1962, p. 7.

⁵ John Fischer, "The Editor's Easy Chair," *Harper's Magazine,* September 1961, pp. 10–16.

⁶ Allan Nevins, *The State Universities and Democracy* (Urbana: University of Illinois Press, 1962), p. 114.

⁷ C. P. Snow, 110th anniversary banquet speech, Washington University, St. Louis, Mo., Feb. 23, 1963.

⁸ Jacques Barzun, *The House of Intellect* (New York: Harper, 1959).

⁹ F. M. Cornford, *Microcosmographia Academica Being a Guide for the Young Academic Politician* (Cambridge, Eng.: Dunster House, 1923), p. 32.

¹⁰ Harold Laski, "The American College President," *Harper's Monthly Magazine,* February 1932, p. 319; Abraham Flexner, *Universities: American English German* (New York: Oxford University Press, 1930), p. 5.

¹¹ Frederick Rudolph, *The American College and University: A History* (New York: Alfred A. Knopf, 1962), p. 491.

¹² Nevitt Sanford, "Higher Education as a Social Problem," in Sanford, ed., *The American College: A Psychological and Social Interpretation of the Higher Learning* (New York: John Wiley & Sons, 1962), p. 19.

¹³ C. P. Snow, *The Masters* (New York: Macmillan, 1951), Appendix, p. 382.

¹⁴ Eric Ashby, "Self-Government in Modern British Universities," *Science and Freedom,* December 1956, p. 10.

¹⁵ Frank Pinner, "The Crisis of the State Universities: Analysis and Remedies," in Sanford, ed., p. 91.

¹⁶ Logan Wilson, *Academic Man* (London: Oxford University Press, 1942), p. 71.

¹⁷ Ashby, p. 5.

¹⁸ *Reports of the Course of Instruction in Yale College by a Committee*

of the Corporation and the Academical Faculty (New Haven, Conn.: Hezekiah Howe, 1828), in *American Journal of Science and Arts,* vol. 15 (January 1829), p. 298.

[19] J. Robert Oppenheimer, "Science and the Human Community," in Charles Frankel, ed., *Issues in University Education* (New York: Harper, 1959), pp. 56, 58.

[20] Beardsley Ruml, *Memo to A College Trustee: A Report on Financial and Structural Problems of the Liberal College* (New York: McGraw-Hill, 1959).

[21] Cornford, p. 4.

[22] James Bryant Conant, *Education in A Divided World* (Cambridge, Mass.: Harvard University Press, 1949), pp. 158, 171.

[23] John Maynard Keynes, *The General Theory* (New York: Harcourt Brace, 1936), p. 383.

[24] David Riesman, *Constraint and Variety in American Education* (Garden City, N.Y.: Doubleday, 1958), p. 33.

[25] C. P. Snow, *The Two Cultures and the Scientific Revolution* (New York: Cambridge University Press, 1959).

[26] Karl Jaspers, *The Idea of the University,* trans. H. A. T. Reiche and H. F. Vanderschmidt (Boston: Beacon Press, 1959), 46.

[27] Sir Walter Moberly, *The Crisis in the University* (London: SCM Press, 1949), p. 20.

[28] George W. Beadle, "The University of X," *Context,* Fall 1961.

[29] Riesman, p. 64.

[30] Lee DuBridge, "The Shape of the Future," *Engineering and Science,* California Institute of Technology, February 1962, p. 13.

[31] Clark Kerr, John T. Dunlop, Frederick H. Harbison, and Charles A. Myers, *Industrialism and Industrial Man* (Cambridge, Mass.: Harvard University Press, 1960).

[32] A. N. Whitehead, *The Aims of Education & Other Essays* (New York: Macmillan, 1929), pp. 22–23.

INDEX

Academic emphases, shift in, 110–113
Acceleration of work, 109
Adams, Charles K., 13
Administration, 27–28; and federal funds, 67; problem of relating to faculty and students, 120
Agricultural Experiment Stations, 52
Agricultural Extension Service, 52
Agriculture, schools of, 15
Alumni, rising sense of concern of, 102–103
American Assembly, 50, 83
American Council on Education, 50
Angell, James B., 13, 33–34
Antoninus, Marcus Aurelius, 32
Argonne Laboratory, 48
Arts, creative, 112
Ashby, Eric, 31, 97, 98
Athletics, 16, 90
Atomic Energy Commission, 54

Bacon, Sir Francis, quoted, 2
Balance, problems of, 55–69, 69–75, 113–114
Barnard, Frederick, 13
Barzun, Jacques, 94
Beadle, George, 122
Berlin, University of, 5, 11
Biology, 111–112
Bologna, University of, 10, 20, 25
Bonaparte, Napoleon, 24, 105
Brookings Institution, 50
Brown University, 13
Bryce, Lord, 32
Bundy, McGeorge, 22, 83
Bureau of Labor Statistics, 76
"Bureaucratic balance," 51, 69–75

Bush, Vannevar, 48
Business administration, schools of, 15
Butler, Nicholas Murray, 33

Calendars, rearrangement of, 109
California, University of: growth, 7–8; Lawrence Radiation Laboratory, 48
Cambridge University, 10, 25, 26; faculty control at, 22; administration, 27, 28; and the faculty guild, 96, 97; research at, 98
Carnegie Foundation, 50
Change: problems of, 106–108; new faces of, 108–118; still to come, 118–123
Chicago, University of, 17; extension programs, 16; Argonne Laboratory, 48
Clark, Burton R., 41
Colleges, U.S., 12; junior, 108
Columbia University, 16
Commons, John R., 16
Compton, Karl T., 48
Conant, James Bryant, 18, 48, 113
Concentration, inevitability of, 63–64
Cornell University, 48
Cornford, F. M., 96, 107
Corson, John J., 20
Council of Advisers on Education, 83

Day, Jeremiah, 22
Department, creation of, 11
Department of Agriculture, 54
Department of Defense, 54
Department of Health, Education and Welfare, 50
Disciplines, unification of, 119–120
Doctors, federal support for training of, 82–83

Dodds, Harold W., 31
Drop-outs, problem of, 76
Dublin, University of, 2
DuBridge, Lee, 123

Elective system, 12, 13, 14, 21–22, 23
Eliot, Charles W., 12, 13, 17, 18, 32, 35
Engineering, schools of, 15
Engineering, Science and Management
    War Training Program, 52
Erasmus, 95
External imperatives, 105–108
Extracurricular programs, 21

Faculty: influence of, 22–23; life in mul-
    tiversity, 42–44; and the un-faculty,
    65–67; competition for, 109–110; sala-
    ries and fringe benefits, 109–110
Faculty guild idea, 95–102
Federal Housing Authority, 81
Federal support: of education, 51–55; of
    scientific research, 48–49, 53–55, 60–
    69; suggestions concerning, 75–84
Flexner, Abraham: on the idea of a uni-
    versity, 4; on Harvard, 5; complaints
    regarding universities, 5–6; on Johns
    Hopkins, 13; and the university as an
    organism, 20; on the university presi-
    dent, 30–31; on the autocratic presi-
    dent, 33; on the professoriat, 44; on
    the conservatism of universities, 96
Folwell, William W., 13
Foundations, 105
France, university patterns in, 93
Franklin, Benjamin, 12
Frondizi, Risieri, 21

Galileo, 95
Germany: rebirth of university in, 11; in-
    fluence on American universities, 18,
    47–48; public control in, 24; faculty
    class structure in, 97
"G.I. Bill," 52

Gilman, Daniel Coit, 13
Gilpatric, Roswell L., 70
Gilpatric report, 70, 89
Göttingen, 11, 12
Governance, multiversity, 18–28
Graduate centers, 109
Graduate fellowship programs, 81–82
Graduate school, development of, 13–14
Great Britain, influence of, 18; "public"
    control in, 25
Growth, university, 108–110

Halle, 11
Harper, William Rainey, 13
Harvard University: Flexner on, 5;
    growth of, 7; Ticknor's attempts to re-
    form, 12; under Eliot, 13; and the land
    grant movement, 15, 48; faculty power
    at, 22, 23; general education program,
    23; self-study, 50, 74; MacLeish on,
    85–86; medical school, 115
Hatch Act (1887), 52
Hofstadter, Richard, 25
Holland, 25
Home economics, 15
Hook, Sidney, 57
House of Intellect, 94
Humboldt, Wilhelm von, 11
Hutchins, Robert M., 17, 23; idea of a
    university, 20; on the university presi-
    dent, 31–32, 33, 40; as last of the gi-
    ants, 33

Ideopolis, rise of, 91–94
Industry, and the universities, 89–91
Informal influences, 26–27
Institute, creation of, 11
Instruction: growing concern with quality
    of, 103–105; mechanization of, 109;
    undergraduate, improvement of, 118–
    119
Intellect, organized, 123–126
"Intuitive imbalance," 51, 55–69

Italy, government control in, 24

Jefferson, Thomas, 12, 21, 34
Johns Hopkins University, 13
Jordan, David Starr, 13, 85
Jowett, Benjamin, 32

Kidd, Charles V., 78
"Knowledge industry," 87–91

Land Grant Association, 72
Land grant movement, 15–16, 46–48
Laski, Harold, 96
Latin America, 26; student power in, 21; government control, in, 24
Lawrence Radiation Laboratory, 48
Lazarsfeld, Paul, 33
Lehrfreiheit, 11, 14, 44
Lernfreiheit, 11, 14, 42
Library, emphasis on, 12
Lincoln, Abraham, 46
Lincoln Laboratory, 48
London, University of, 5–6
Lowell, A. Lawrence, 16–17, 18, 32

Machlup, Fritz, 88
MacLeish, Archibald, 85
Marcus Aurelius. *See* Antoninus
Marx, Karl, 125
Massachusetts Institute of Technology, 115; Lincoln Laboratory, 48; location, 89
Michigan, University of, 13, 15
Mill, John Stuart, 96
Millett, John D., 31
Morality, campus, 106
Morrill, James L., 31
Morrill Act (1862), 15, 46, 51
Morrill Act, Second (1890), 51
Multiversity: historical origins of, 9–18; governance of, 18–28; life in, 41–45

Name, importance of, 19–20

Napoleon. *See* Bonaparte
NASA (National Aeronautics and Space Administration), 54, 71
National Defense Education Act, 57, 71, 81
National Defense Research Committee, 52
National Education Improvement Act, proposed, 70
National Foundation for Higher Education, 80–81
National Institutes of Health, 54, 71, 82
National Science Foundation, 54, 71, 81, 82
National Youth Administration, 52
Nevins, Allan, 15, 35, 91
Newman, Cardinal, 2–3
Newton, Isaac, 95
Nobel Prize winners, concentration of, 91, 92
Northwest Ordinance of 1785, 51

Office of Scientific Research and Development, 52
Oppenheimer, Robert S., 101
Orlans, Harold, 64, 77
Ortega y Gassett, José, 21
Oxford University, 10, 25, 26, 96, 97, 98; faculty control at, 22; administration, 27, 28

Paris, University of, 10, 22, 25
Pennsylvania, University of, 12
Philadelphia, College of. *See* Pennsylvania, University of
Plato, 9
President, university, 29–36; as mediator, 36–41
President's Science Advisory Committee, 50, 72
Price, Don K., 48, 69
Princeton University, 13, 50

Problems of change, 105–108
Professions, shifting emphasis in needs for, 111
Professor, established as great figure, 11
Project system, 77–80
Public authority, 24–26
Pusey, Nathan, 6, 69
Pythagoreans, 9

Rashdall, Hastings, 10
Research funds, federal, 53–55
Riesman, David, 39, 122
Rockefeller Foundation, 82
ROTC program, 52
Rudolph, Frederick, 31, 34, 96
Ruml, Beardsley, 106
Russia, 24; as spur to scientific revolution, 49; university development patterns in, 93

Salaries, faculty, 109, 110
Salerno, 10
Sanford, Nevitt, 97
Schumpeter, Joseph, 34
Scientific research, federal support of, 48–49, 53–55, 60–69
Seaborg report, 70
Sinclair, Upton, 31
Smith-Lever Act (1914), 52
Snow, C. P., 91, 97, 119
Sophists, 8, 9
Spain, student power in, 21
Sports. *See* Athletics
Stanford Research Institute, 90
Sterling Forest, 89
Stratton, Julius A., 67
Students, 20–22; multiversity, 41–42; teaching graduate vs. teaching undergraduate, 64–65; undergraduate, restlessness in, 103–105

Talent, concentration of, 91–93
Tappan, Henry, 13, 17; Angell on, 33–34
Teaching, of undergraduates vs. graduates, 64–65. *See also* Instruction
Ticknor, Professor George, 12
Trow, Martin, 41

United States, development of university in, 12
Universities: evolution of, 4–9; 18th-century European, 10–11; American, second transformation of, 86–94; clichés concerning, 94; growth of, 108–110; involvement in life of society, 114–118
University Grants Committee (British), 72, 105

Van Hise, Charles, 16
Veblen, Thorstein, 31
Virginia, University of, 12

Wallis, Alen, 59
Washington, professors in, 115
Wayland, Francis, 13, 34
Weinberg, Alvin M., 78
Wheeler, Benjamin Ide, 13, 33, 34
White, Andrew Dickson, 13
Whitehead, Alfred North, 126
Wilson, Logan, 69
Wilson, Woodrow, 34
Wisconsin, University of, 16
"Wisconsin Idea," 16, 21
Woodrow Wilson Foundation, 82
Work Projects Administration, 52
Wriston, Henry M., 31

Yale University, 99; in 1828, 12–13; elective system at, 13, 14; faculty power at, 22